POVERTY PROPAGANDA
Exploring the myths

Tracy Shildrick

WITHDRAWN

P

First published in Great Britain in 2018 by

Policy Press
University of Bristol
1-9 Old Park Hill
Bristol
BS2 8BB
UK
t: +44 (0)117 954 5940
pp-info@bristol.ac.uk
www.policypress.co.uk

North America office:
Policy Press
c/o The University of Chicago Press
1427 East 60th Street
Chicago, IL 60637, USA
t: +1 773 702 7700
f: +1 773-702-9756
sales@press.uchicago.edu
www.press.uchicago.edu

British Library Cataloguing in Publication Data
A catalogue record for this book is available from the British Library

Library of Congress Cataloging-in-Publication Data
A catalog record for this book has been requested

ISBN 978-1-4473-2398-3 paperback
ISBN 978-1-4473-2397-6 hardcover
ISBN 978-1-4473-2401-0 ePub
ISBN 978-1-4473-2402-7 Mobi
ISBN 978-1-4473-2400-3 ePdf

Cover design by Lyn Davies
Printed and bound in Great Britain by CPI Group (UK) Ltd,
Croydon, CR0 4YY
Policy Press uses environmentally responsible print partners

Contents

List of abbreviations

CPAG	Child Poverty Action Group
DfE	Department for Education
DWP	Department for Work and Pensions
EHRC	Equality and Human Rights Commission
EU	European Union
IFS	Institute for Fiscal Studies
JRF	Joseph Rowntree Foundation
JSA	Jobseeker's Allowance
NHS	National Health Service
ONS	Office for National Statistics
TUC	Trades Union Congress

Acknowledgements

In writing this book I owe various debts of gratitude to family, friends and colleagues who have all been supportive in different ways. Robert MacDonald, the late Andy Furlong, Colin Webster, Kayleigh Garthwaite, Johann Roden and Robert Crow were all co-researchers on the various research projects referred to in the book. The research participants in all of those projects deserve a special mention for sharing their lives with such honesty and generosity. Particular thanks go to Anqi Shen and also to Ruth Patrick, Pauline Ramshaw, Louise Wattis, Anthony Ruddy and Georgios Papanicoloau. The occasional meet-ups really helped but we really ought to try and do it more often! Robert Crow at Teesside remained a loyal and reliable supporter of the work and his ability to find sometimes obscure material never ceased to amaze me. Sharon Elley at Leeds was generous with her careful proof-reading skills. Adrian Sinfield has provided no end of valuable source material as well as commenting on various ideas and drafts of the book. He and his wife, Dorothy, have supported the research in lots of different ways over recent years and I feel incredibly privileged to have benefited from their immense knowledge, kindness and hospitality. Policy Press has been endlessly patient and tolerant and particular thanks go to Ali Shaw who continued to believe in me and in the value of the book, even when I occasionally didn't! The ideas benefited enormously from the debates I had with my level three Leeds SSP undergraduate students studying the 'Class in Everyday Life' module in early 2017. Most importantly, my family have continued to support and believe in me. Looking back, it is hard to believe that my daughters, Jessica and Chelsea, were just babies when I embarked on my undergraduate degree as a mature student at Teesside University. They have grown into two exceptional young women who continue to indulge my 'poverty passion' with both patience and grace, and I will forever be enormously proud of them both. Finally, my husband Steve never stopped believing in my ability to complete the book and he has generously tolerated my (very) many evening and weekend absences with love and little complaint. I owe a lot to people who have supported me, but of course, the book and any flaws in it are all my own.

ONE

Introduction

> The issue of people moving repeatedly between work and
> unemployment is an endemic problem in the UK and has
> risen by 60 per cent since 2006, mostly as a result of the
> recession. Entering work cannot provide a sustainable route
> out of poverty if job security, low pay and lack of progression
> are not also addressed. (Goulden, 2010, p 1)

Evidence shows that poverty, and the insecurity that inevitably
accompanies it, is affecting the lives of more and more ordinary
working-age people and families, not just in Britain and the UK
more broadly but also across the globe (Standing, 2010; 2014; 2016).
Poverty has become a normalised aspect of day-to-day life for millions
of individuals and families in Britain today, yet it occupies a peculiar
and contradictory position in both popular and political debates.
Poverty is widespread in Britain, as well as in the UK more broadly,
and all indications show that its incidence, particularly for children
and working-age households, will continue to rise under the current
direction of policy (Hood and Waters, 2017). Poverty in Britain is
most often caused by 'poor work' (Byrne, 2005) – that is, work that
fails to take people away from poverty either for long enough or
far enough to make a difference to their lives – and by inadequate
'welfare', particularly for those forced to rely on out-of-work benefits
(JRF, 2016). More and more people find themselves trapped between
the two as they cycle in and out of short-term, low-paid work and
on and off inadequate (and increasingly difficult to access) 'welfare'
payments. Yet the low-pay, no-pay cycle, as it is often referred to, still
remains a relative blind spot in political and policy debates. Since 2010,
cuts forced through in the name of austerity have also added to the
problem, although the general trends towards increasing inequality and
diminishing opportunities for those who are economically marginalised
go back much further than the recession of 2008 and the subsequent
imposition of numerous cuts. Yet, despite the widespread existence
of poverty in Britain, it is all too frequently ignored, increasingly
demonised and, when it is discussed, almost always presented in
ways that are misleading and inaccurate. As a result, poverty both as

a concept and as a condition, is generally misunderstood and it is this misunderstanding and misrepresentation that this book aims to address.

This book argues that poverty propaganda – deliberately and often very carefully crafted myths and misrepresentations about poverty and those who experience the condition – has the biggest influence on how poverty is understood in the contemporary context. Poverty propaganda works to ensure that myths and false pronouncements about poverty and its causes and consequences are disseminated widely: thus poverty is at one and the same time both increasingly a normalised condition in contemporary Britain and also one that is demonised to such as degree that its real causes and consequences are barely discussed. Such is the strength of stigma and shame that comes from this misrepresentation that even those experiencing deep poverty and related disadvantages do everything they can to distance themselves from the condition (Shildrick and MacDonald, 2013). One of the reasons why poverty propaganda is so successful is not simply its ability to disguise poverty but its capacity to stigmatise not just those people who are experiencing poverty, but whole swathes of often very loosely defined segments of society who are in some way disadvantaged. It is precisely this woolliness in the target populations of poverty propaganda that makes its messages so powerful and that ensures that poverty as a condition can continue to be largely overlooked. Neoliberal regimes, such as that which has dominated in Britain since the mid-1970s, provide fertile ground for poverty propaganda to flourish as life chances are increasingly presented as – and largely understood to be – the sole responsibility of individuals (Beck, 2002). Neoliberal capitalist regimes are predicated on the promotion of widespread improvements in living conditions and the increasing availability of opportunities for personal and economic advancement. The language of the day might change, but the British equivalent of the 'American dream', whether it be in the form of the 'the opportunity society' (Major, 1991) or the latest incarnation in the form of 'The Great Meritocracy' (May, 2017), holds a special place in the British public's psyche and does much to help overshadow the gross and growing inequalities in access to opportunities that blight the lives and potential of increasing numbers of people.

Poverty propaganda not only hides the structural causes of poverty but also feeds negative, stigmatising and discriminatory attitudes towards those who are experiencing the condition. It allows punitive and sometimes downright cruel policies to be enacted towards those experiencing the condition, and for those policies to be largely tolerated by a public that buys into the rhetoric of poverty propaganda and thus accepts – and sometimes demands – that those believed to be underserving are punished. It has long been known that people experiencing poverty tend to be powerless and voiceless (Lister, 2004). Yet, what is so effective and powerful about poverty propaganda is that it works to stigmatise the disadvantaged with such vigour and venom that even those experiencing deep poverty and other disadvantages go to great lengths to distance themselves and their own lives from the condition.

Alongside this proliferation of rhetoric and propaganda about poverty we see charities, campaigners and a growing number of academics continuing to raise concerns about the existence of poverty in Britain and its growth, particularly since 2010, under recent government policy decisions. In the UK official measures of poverty tend to use relative definitions of poverty and Peter Townsend's understanding of relative poverty has been widely influential:

> Individuals, families and groups in the population can be said to be in poverty when they lack resources to obtain the type of diet, participate in the activities and have the living conditions and amenities which are customary, or at least widely encouraged and approved, in the societies in which they belong. (Townsend, 1979, p 31)

Thus, poverty can be understood as having 'resources that are so seriously below those commanded by the average individual or family that they are, in effect, excluded from ordinary living patterns, customs and activities' (Townsend, 1979, p 31). In 2016 the Joseph Rowntree Foundation (JRF) released its anti-poverty strategy and estimated that 13.5 million people in the UK were living in poverty, with the figure predicted to rise under current government policies (JRF, 2016). The strategy was ground breaking in both its breadth and its ambition. The JRF argues that:

> The level of poverty in the UK is shameful. This should be a place where everyone can achieve a decent, secure standard of living. Instead, millions of people – many from working families – are struggling to meet their needs. (JRF, 2016, p 5)

This book is mostly concerned with poverty in Britain, but the main arguments are ones that resonate much more widely, not just across the UK but also across the United States (US) and many Western European countries. Since the mid-1970s Britain has pursued a socio-political agenda not dissimilar to the US in terms of generating stark economic inequalities in life chances and life experiences for its citizens, with particularly difficult conditions being wrought on those at the bottom of the socio-economic structure.

It has been an overriding interest in issues of economic inequality and the disparities of life opportunities and life chances that has dominated my 20-or-so-year career in sociology. It was my puzzlement at both the existence of inequalities and, perhaps especially, the lack of resistance to them that inspired an initial decision to leave a career in nursing and to pursue further study as a mature student. My grandad's stories of his early life, lived in deep poverty in what were then some of the most deprived parts of the East End of London, sparked my developing sociological imagination as a young adult. Grandad was raised by a single mother who was widowed at an early age and who, before the inception of the welfare state, had to raise nine children alone and worked three different cleaning jobs in order that the family could simply survive. Grandad, like a minority of children from disadvantaged backgrounds in that era (1930s), passed the 11-plus and was accepted into grammar school. He took up his place and, despite all of the emotional and financial upheaval it cost him and his mother, he didn't stick it. His embarrassment in the context of most of his peers who didn't make it to grammar school was so acute that he described to me how he would frantically struggle out of his school uniform two streets away from the block of flats where they lived in order that it would not be seen by the other children. In the end it was not his sense of being out of place that finished his grammar school education but the financial pressures at home. He left school and went to work down on the docks. Interestingly, my grandad never relayed this story with any sense of injustice, even if that was how it resonated with me. Grandad saw it as his duty and responsibility to help the family budget, and I'm certain that he felt more at home down on the docks than he ever did at the grammar school.

Grandad married my nana and they moved from the south to the north-east of England, where Nana had been born and raised. They bought their own home after moving from their council house and stayed there all of their lives. Nana worked part-time, mostly in cleaning jobs, for much of their marriage, and Grandad worked for various large companies, including British Steel and ICI, working his way up to a relatively senior role in the chemical laboratories. My grandparents lived relatively stable working and working-class lives, neither in poverty nor in luxury, for the whole of their lives. Nana still lives in their little bungalow at the grand age of 97 and often reminds the form of out-of-work benefits. Poverty propaganda rests on an individualistic explanation of life chances and life experiences, and thus the structural explanations and drivers of poverty are clouded out. The current context is one where poverty propaganda thrives and becomes ever more powerful as neo-liberal capitalist regimes, such as that which has been operating in Britain over the last forty years, orchestrate a view of life and life chances that prioritises individual responsibility over structural conditions and drivers that cause poverty. Rising general standards of living and overt discourses that have openly denied the existence of poverty have all worked to foster fertile ground for the proliferation of poverty propaganda.

Language lies at the heart of poverty propaganda; but, as we will see through the pages of this book, poverty propaganda has real effects on both the existence of poverty and the ways in which people experiencing poverty are treated and feel about their own lives. Poverty propaganda presents a picture of both the causes and consequences of poverty that stands in opposition to the realities of poverty, but its messages are so simple that they appear to makes sense to many people, and thus have in many respects become common sense. Part of the appeal of poverty propaganda and the reason why it is frequently accepted as truth is that it makes effective use of ready and easily digested caricatures. Easily understood sound bites work to create a very distinct perception of 'us' and 'them', with those experiencing poverty or related disadvantages being relegated to a very distinctive 'other' (Lister, 2004). Ready sound bites such as the 'shirkers' and the 'strivers' or 'hard-working families' are used to evoke feelings of unfairness in the system (particularly the 'welfare' system). The language shifts over time; so, in more recent times, we have heard a lot about 'families who have never worked' and the idea of 'intergenerational cultures of worklessness', along with 'troubled families', but essentially all of these ideas portray poverty as the preserve of the undeserving who are culpable for their own fate.

The messages of poverty propaganda are diffuse and are threaded through policy and political and popular discourse in a way that ensures that they have clarity and consistency. As we will see in below and in Chapter Seven, the focus and language of policy documents has shifted in recent years, particularly since 2010, towards a 'social problem' focus. The welfare state has been increasingly depicted as problematic, leading to supposed 'welfare dependency'. Structural drivers of poverty, such as unemployment and inadequate out-of-work benefits, are rarely cited as contemporary causes of poverty, with more emphasis being given to 'welfare dependency' (DWP, 2010; 2015; 2016), whereby those in receipt of out-of-work benefits are depicted as losing a willingness to work because of the security of those benefits. 'Troubled families' have also received significant amounts of attention, becoming, as we will see below, the sole focus of work around 'social justice' under the Coalition government elected in 2010. What all of these discourses produce is a problem-focused analysis, whereby social problems such as unemployment become problems that can be explained by the behaviour of those experiencing the problem and the structural causes of poverty can be conveniently removed from view.

These issues are then reworked in popular and political discourses, perpetuating the view that those experiencing poverty are undeserving of support and culpable for their own situations. Periodic announcements from powerful senior political figures frequently refer to the welfare state as purely meaning out-of-work benefits and depict the system as variously 'broken' or 'failing' and as being responsible for producing generations of work-shy families (see Shildrick et al, 2012b). At other times generic depictions are drawn on (as happened after the riots in 2011) to decry sections of society that are deemed to be deviant and problematic and to extend and deepen generic narratives of the work-shy and underserving that were already well embedded in popular and political discourses. It is the malleability of poverty propaganda that makes it particularly powerful and effective. Generic populations are implicated in its stigmatising narratives, from those living in social housing to people with life-limiting illnesses who are forced to rely on out-of-work benefits. It is this diffuse and indiscriminate nature of poverty propaganda that makes it so effective and powerful.

Newspapers, in particular the tabloid press, play a crucial role in propagating poverty propaganda and adding to its weight by producing sometimes outrageous headlines that reinforce the notion that some people are work-shy, lazy and 'getting something for nothing'. These depictions of people experiencing poverty and related disadvantages have become particularly prominent through television programmes of the genre referred to as 'poverty porn'. These programmes, perhaps best exemplified by *Benefits Street* (made by Love Productions and first aired in 2014), present people experiencing poverty in ways that reinforce individualised understandings of poverty and the idea that people are somehow culpable for their own predicament. As such, the programmes are very good examples of how poverty propaganda works.

Poverty propaganda successfully constructs generic but very powerful narratives around poverty and related disadvantage and the people who experience it. Its rhetoric successfully obscures the real causes of poverty that are structural and related to the lack of opportunities for decent-paying, secure work and the low rates of UK out-of-work benefits (JRF, 2016). Poverty propaganda also distorts the realities of living with poverty or surviving on out-of-work benefits, along with the realities of struggling to make ends meet through low-paid employment. Significantly, the almost complete focus on individual behaviours obscures the importance of intergenerational disadvantage and the role of social class in advantaging some people while severely limiting the life chances of others (Bloodworth, 2016). According to Stanley (2015) in his account of how propaganda works,

> When societies are unjust, for example in the distribution of wealth, we can expect the emergence of flawed ideologies. The flawed ideologies allow for effective propaganda. In a society that is unjust, due to unjust distinctions between persons, ways of rationalizing undeserved privilege become ossified into rigid and unchangeable belief. These beliefs are barriers to rational thought and empathy that propaganda exploits. (p 3)

Poverty propaganda is not necessarily simply rhetoric or mythology, although as we will learn in this chapter the two form a significant part of it. It will often start from a 'kernel of truth' (Stanley, 2015, p 3), but then spiral outwards, manipulating the truth and building narratives that cloud out reality and that stereotype and misrepresent the causes and consequences of poverty. The success of poverty propaganda paves the way for punitive policies that can be directed towards those experiencing poverty. The recent austerity agenda that has been pursued with vigour since 2010 is a very good example whereby conditions of life for those on the lowest incomes have been deliberately worsened. For Cooper and Whyte (2017), austerity is a 'class project that disproportionately targets and affects working class households' (p 11). Yet, poverty propaganda effectively obscures these realities, worsening life conditions and opportunities for many, while ensuring that the general public largely accepts these developments. Chapter Seven discusses further the purpose and consequences of poverty propaganda.

'Welfare' as supporting and driving poverty

Myths and grossly misleading statements about 'welfare' have become the lynchpin around which many other elements of poverty propaganda coalesce. 'Welfare' has been rebranded in the present context to refer principally to out-of-work benefits, while a broader and more accurate understanding would indicate that out-of-work benefits make up only a small proportion of the total 'welfare' bill and, indeed, that almost every citizen benefits from 'welfare' of one sort or another (Hills, 2015). Yet this broader, more accurate understanding of what constitutes 'welfare' and how it benefits people across society is drowned out by an overwhelming and concerted focus on 'welfare' as pertaining only to claimants of out-of-work benefits, such as sickness benefit or Jobseeker's Allowance. Of course, those who receive out-of-work benefits are an important group if we want to properly understand poverty in Britain, as the levels of out-of-work benefit mean that those receiving them and who rely on them for their income are in deep poverty (JRF, 2016). Yet accounts of the hardship of living on out-of-work benefits are rarely aired, while stories about people supposedly living well for free dominate the popular and political conversation. Supplemented by the corresponding narrative of people on out-of-work benefits being 'welfare dependent', work-shy and in general undeserving (Shildrick and MacDonald, 2013; Patrick, 2016; Garthwaite, 2016b), these ideas are employed with the specific aim of invoking public outrage towards the welfare state and those in receipt of out-of-work benefits (Jensen, 2014; Allen et al, 2015; Jensen and Tyler, 2015).

In Chapter Seven we will read about the crafting of poverty propaganda and the power of political and policy discourses in shaping debates more generally (as well as feeding the direction of policy itself). The media, and in particular the tabloid media, plays a strong role in supporting and driving these divisive, dysfunctional and false depictions of life on out-of-work benefits. The tabloid media regularly run front-page news items that play to the 'scrounger' narrative with attention-grabbing, silly and sometimes downright fantastical headlines. For example, 'Jobless man who used a food bank after blowing his benefits in a casino blames the government for giving him a "ridiculous" amount of money in one go' (*Daily Mail*, 2015b) and 'Not too fat to bat: Too fat to work scrounger plays beach cricket with his wife as he recovers from a mini-stroke brought on by "overwork"' (*Daily Mail*, 2015c). Despite the wealth of evidence to the contrary, these sorts of stories are rolled out with increasing regularity as a way of manufacturing 'common sense' ideas about 'welfare' and poverty (Jensen, 2014) and to create stereotypes of those experiencing the condition.

The UK has followed a similar path to what occurred in the US, whereby the so-called 'welfare queens' came to powerfully epitomise everything that was deemed to be wrong with the 'welfare' system, paving the way for the introduction of workfare and conditionality.

During the 1970s President Ronald Reagan repeatedly employed the rhetoric of the 'welfare queen' to argue that 'welfare' was overly generous and open to exploitation (Allen et al, 2015). It was at this point during anti-welfare-fraud campaigns in the US that the 'racialised caricature of the "welfare queen"' entered the political lexicon (Kohler-Hausmann, 2015, p 756). Lawrence Mead was the key protagonist behind the introduction of punitive workfare measures in the US and he was vocal as to why, in his view, punitive 'welfare' reforms were needed:

> Once, the most divisive demands on government were inspired by the working class; they now arise from the nonworking underclass ...//... personal responsibility must be willed, precisely because it can no longer be assumed. It must become an explicit policy because it is no longer, as in the progressive era, the unspoken ground of the political culture. Social policy must resist passive poverty justly but firmly – just as the West contained communism – until sanity breaks in and the opposed system collapses of its own weight. (Mead, 1993, pp 1 and 261)

Yet, empirical evidence that supports the notion that people prefer not to work and to rely on 'welfare' is very difficult indeed to come by. Furthermore, there is a significant and growing body of research that shows that people in receipt of 'welfare' and who are able to work (and also those with long-term illnesses who are unable to work or who would struggle to hold down a full-time job) would prefer to be in jobs (Webster et al, 2004; MacDonald and Marsh, 2005; Smith, 2005; Rogaly and Taylor, 2009; Shildrick et al, 2010). The overwhelming weight of evidence from those on very low incomes and wholly reliant on out-of-work benefits for their income shows that people prefer to be in jobs. This is not simply idle rhetoric or a case of giving the most morally palatable answers to researchers but is evidenced by accounts of decades-long, sometimes life-time, commitments to working in 'poor work'.

Commitment to work is consistent and is not just driven by economic necessity and the low level of state benefits or the punitive 'welfare' system; it is also very much related to class and cultural expectations that, historically, have meant that paid employment is deemed to be the best way to afford a decent working-class life (Webster et al, 2004; Smith, 2005; Shildrick et al, 2012a; McIvor, 2013). A key motivation for the 'cultures of worklessness' study mentioned in the Introduction was the failure, over a series of studies undertaken over many years and in some of Teesside's most deprived neighbourhoods, to find people who had never had a job. We have written elsewhere about the changing economy on Teesside (these issues are discussed further in Chapter Four of this book), but across all of the studies, even involving some of the most deprived families in the UK, finding people who had never had jobs was very, very difficult indeed (Shildrick et al, 2012a; 2012b).

Myths about 'welfare' and the supposedly work-shy have a power and an appeal and partly because of their simplicity (Shildrick et al, 2012b). The general public might be forgiven for assuming that these explanations have value, given the number of times that the general ideas appear and their different guises and formats. The idea of families where no one has ever had a job, or whole neighbourhoods that have never worked, is perhaps the epitome of poverty propaganda. It is not only expansive in terms of who might be ensnared in its net, but it can be easily be manipulated to exploit its potential to onerously and negatively label people without jobs. It is frighteningly easy to shift the notion of three generations without jobs to four, as the then Minister for Work and Pensions did on the BBC's *Newsnight* programme on 15 February 2011. Mythological tropes and sound bites like this hold appeal precisely because they can be moulded one way or another to ratchet up the volume of poverty propaganda. Gaffney points out that

> There are two pervasive myths about welfare in the UK which are routinely repeated by politicians and the media. The first is the myth of the family where 'nobody has worked for generations'. The second is the myth of the area where 'nobody works round here'. By 'myths' I don't just mean widely believed falsehoods but statements which embody a mythological mode of thinking which has no relation to facts whatsoever. (Gaffney, 2014)

Jensen and Tyler employ the concept of 'welfare broods' (2015, p 470) to describe the ways in which specific, often extreme, examples of criminality or other forms of deviance are used to produce anti-welfare sentiments. They argue that

> Through the 'crisis lens' the welfare state was re-imagined as fostering toxic forms of 'welfare dependency' amongst citizens, itself considered to have a stagnating effect on economic growth and national prosperity. In a stunning reversal of the 1940s 'welfare imaginary', welfare came to be understood across a wide range of political, social

and cultural milieus as a *cause* of poverty and social problems: including 'inter-generational worklessness', drug dependence, anti-social behaviours, 'troubled families', teenage parenthood, crime and other 'social ills'. (Jensen and Tyler, 2015, p 472)

Jensen and Tyler have looked at the case of Mick Philpot as an example of an extreme case of benefits crime (the manslaughter of his six children when he set light to his home in an elaborate plot to try to gain custody of his children from his ex-girlfriend). The case plays to long-standing prejudices about large families and single parenthood, and the concept of the 'benefit brood' family (Jensen and Tyler, 2015, p 474). Jensen and Tyler cite the clear and forceful use of emotive headlines and imagery, such as this from the *Daily Mail*, where the headline 'Vile product of welfare UK' is presented in very large writing with the smaller (but still clearly visible) accompanying lines, 'Man who bred 17 babies by 5 women to milk benefits system is guilty of killing 6 of them' (Jensen and Tyler, 2015, p 474). Politicians – in particular the former Chancellor, George Osborne (responsible for widespread cuts to 'welfare'), and the then Prime Minister, David Cameron – quickly seized on this extreme example to add weight to their claims that there was something wrong with the welfare state and that it needed to be fixed. George Osborne pointedly asked why the state should be 'subsidising lives like these' (Osborne, 2014) and the *Daily Mail* took the opportunity to loudly denounce Philpott as a 'vile product of welfare UK' (Dolan, 2013). This is a good example of how political figures and their power and influence can be used in tandem with a complicit media to construct and reinforce poverty propaganda. This deliberate opportunism is certainly illustrative of a 'longer history of neoliberal experimentation, policy-making and thinking, whereby the underlying problem to be solved in post-industrial states is the condition of "welfare dependency"' (Jensen and Tyler, 2015, p 477). It is also a very clear example of the clever association of issues (crime and 'welfare') that crafts a powerful and effective form of poverty propaganda that can morph or be moulded to suit the political and economic issues of the day. An extreme, rare and highly emotive and shocking crime such as this one can be shamelessly utilised to reinforce the message that the welfare state is supporting, if not producing, a criminal underclass.

The rise of so-called 'poverty porn' in the UK media, including television, has served in many ways to cement the notion that those on out-of-work benefits are feckless. Programme makers produce films that are claimed to be 'real life' portrayals of life on the economic margins, while critics point to the carefully selected footage that presents the programme participants in particular ways and tends to focus on the unusual rather than the usual. Jensen (2014) argues that poverty porn serves to 'embed new forms of "common sense" about "welfare" and worklessness'. Other, more critical perspectives that might deliver a more accurate account of worklessness and poverty are submerged under perspectives that depict 'welfare' claimants in negative and stereotypical ways. *Benefits Street* is the programme that has, quite rightly, attracted much critical commentary. The programme seemed to ignite the public imagination around 'welfare', and the debate that ensued was extensive and, at times, heated and vitriolic. Of course, the programme tapped into a web of poverty propaganda that was already circulating and well embedded in the public imaginary. Consequently, for many people, the programme simply reported what most felt they already knew: that those on out-of-work benefits were somehow undeserving and personally culpable for their plight. With its larger-than-life characters and quite often tragic story lines, the programme was also very watchable, but it played on themes of class demonisation and 'welfare' stereotyping. As Tyler points out:

> The opening sequence of *Benefit[s] Street* transports its audience into the powerful political imaginary of 'Broken Britain'. From the programme title, *Benefit[s] Street*, through to the montage of images of rubbish-strewn streets, unattended children, loitering youths, cigarettes and alcohol, hooded tops and baseball caps, interposed by a soundtrack of 'unemployed, unemployed, unemployed', the audience is instructed to reimagine the welfare state as a 'benefits culture' that impoverishes citizens, feeds addictions and creates what government ministers describe as fatal dependencies. (Tyler, 2015, p 494)

Benefits Street aside, there are many programmes that play to negative class labelling and stereotyping. *Jeremy Kyle* is a long-standing and popular day-time television programme that publicly dissects the complex problems of people who 'display a total lack of the kind of cultural capital that might moderate the behaviour of others on television, but they also appear to be entirely bereft of the sorts of social capital that might assist them in finding solutions to their problems' (McKendrick et al, 2008, p 36). Similarly popular but highly patronising offerings come in the form of programmes like *The Fairy Job Mother*, where a sanctimonious Hayley Taylor humiliates and exposes individual foibles and failings as a way of trying to get people into jobs, reinforcing the idea of personal failure as a way of explaining unemployment and people's reliance on out-of-work benefits. The jobs market or the structural drivers of unemployment are never mentioned; instead there is a deliberate and at times downright cruel focus on attempts to alter individuals' behaviours as a means of getting them into work. Thus, just as in the US, we find ourselves in the situation whereby 'welfare' has become a 'dirty word' (Gordon, 1998). Carefully crafted discourses of *'welfare' doom* feed a broader process of class stereotyping and class prejudice that serves to manipulate poverty as a condition and that completely reshapes the ways in which out-of-work benefit claimants are understood.

From social justice to 'broken Britain' and those terrible 'troubled families'

As noted above, 'welfare' and, particularly, out-of-work benefits have taken central stage in the production of poverty propaganda. A significant development in these debates and discussions has been the move towards prioritising troubles and troubling behaviours as being at the core of the poverty and disadvantage problem (Crossley, 2017). Increasingly the workless and those experiencing poverty and related disadvantages are deemed not just as work-shy but to be engaged in any number of problematic behaviours, from eating too much, to drinking problematically or taking drugs. Poverty propaganda narratives can be ratcheted up at particular points in time; for example, when particularly punitive policies are being brought forward, poverty propaganda can take on a correspondingly particular focus, such as around the 'benefits cap' or housing benefit.

The notion of 'troubled families' is a good example of the ways in which rhetoric can be employed in particular ways to shape social issues and people's understanding of them. Almost overnight the then Coalition government and Iain Duncan Smith (the then Secretary of State for Work and Pensions) shifted a concern for social justice –at that time a relatively new phrase that was being adopted in political and policy arenas (United Nations, 2006) – to a concern with deeply troubled families and individuals. Cleverly, social injustice was able to masquerade as social justice. Rawls (2003) writes that social justice is essentially about 'justice as fairness' and the protection of equal access to liberties, rights and opportunities. Prior to the publication of the report *Social justice: Transforming lives* (DWP, 2012), the Coalition government put out a call for evidence. With colleagues, I responded to the call, stressing the importance of decent work opportunities and barriers that inhibit what I understand by social justice. No doubt others will have flagged similar themes. Yet the report, when it appeared, completely reframed a concern for social justice with a focus on very troubled families. Duncan Smith set the tone of the report in its opening statement. Drawing on a report that he had apparently received from a charity, he referred to a graphic and disturbing photograph of children in a room with their drug-addicted parents. Referring to the caption that accompanies the photograph, it is noted:

> The house of children whose parents are addicted to crack cocaine. Dad has passed out on the mattress in his own vomit. Mum is crouched over a table preparing her fix. What you don't see is the children hidden in the corner crying. (DWP, 2012, p 1)

The stereotyping and class-prejudice work being done here is very easy to decode. The graphic depiction is meant to evoke an emotional response. The specific example is deliberately emotive, aimed to shock. But the evidence shows that this sort of case is very rare. Thus, the depiction is clearly sensationalist. It is meant to be both evocative and provocative and to cement in place powerful and persuasive ideas about poverty and its causes. The evidence shows that only a small proportion of poverty is associated with problem substance misuse. Yet Duncan Smith continues by writing that this is 'not an isolated case' and, furthermore, 'in the UK today there are hundreds of thousands of families living profoundly troubled lives' (DWP, 2012, p 1). This was an important moment in the history of poverty propaganda. Almost overnight the troubled family moved from the periphery of conversations to the centre, aptly aided and supported by the convenience of the rioting that had taken place just a year earlier. Announcing new investment and a determination to deal with the supposed problem, Prime Minister David Cameron had argued that:

> Officialdom might call them 'families with multiple disadvantages'. Some in the press might call them 'neighbours from hell'. Whatever you call them, we've known for years that a relatively small number of families are the source of a large proportion of the problems in society. Drug addiction, alcohol abuse, crime, a culture

of disruption and irresponsibility that cascades through generations. (Cameron, 2011)

Louise Casey, the so-called 'troubled families czar', was given space to develop what became known as the flagship Troubled Families Programme. In the space of just over a year, the programme went from being lauded as having almost 100% success to being proved via evaluation in 2016 to be a complete and utter failure. The warnings of academics (Levitas, 2012; Crossley, 2015, 2016; Portas, 2016) and the problems identified with the direction of travel were completely ignored.

Elsewhere I provide a more detailed discussion of the issue of 'troubled families' (Shildrick et al, 2016) but for our purposes here two key things are important to note: firstly, the volume of publicity given to Casey and her small-scale report that detailed accounts of very troubled families' lives. Her work was given multiple platforms across mainstream news reports, popular discussion programmes and the like. For a while Casey was everywhere, and as a consequence the issue of 'troubled families', and the 'truly appalling' (Casey, 2012) aspects of their lives were traipsed across as many mainstream media outlets as possible. It was of little matter that families such as those that Casey spoke with and of the sort that feature in our intergenerational cultures of worklessness research are rare: they became a key focus of discussion and policy development. The focus on so-called 'troubled families' served a political purpose in so far as it exaggerated and amplified a particular and complex set of problems while allowing the far more prevalent problems of poverty or in-work poverty, for example, to be largely ignored. Little wonder, then, that the policy response was doomed to utter failure (Portas, 2016).

Poverty as associated with excessive and problematic drug use, alcohol use or other supposedly feckless and irresponsible behaviour is a recurrent theme in discussions about poverty. Periodically, sensationalist cases and stories surface in the media about the apparent scale of 'welfare' being given to people with drug-addiction problems or other issues such as obesity. David Cameron drew attention to the issue in 2015 when he suggested that those with problems such as drug or alcohol issues or obesity might have their benefits cut if they refused treatment (Cameron, 2015). Such pronouncements play to the long-standing inference that some people are not worthy of support and that they are lazy and unwilling to help themselves. By deliberately manipulating facts and taking isolated or unusual cases and making out that they are the norm, politicians like Cameron stoke the fires of poverty propaganda. These pronouncements provide ready fodder for the tabloid press that regularly seizes on the bizarre and sometimes downright ridiculous to produce snappy headlines designed to invoke outrage at the welfare state. For example, 'Couple "too fat to work" marry in wedding costing £3000, including buffet from a kebab shop' (*Mirror*, 2015a) and 'Too fat to work: 26 stone mum and her 17 stone daughter claim £30,000 benefits' (*Mirror*, 2015b). These stories play to a class and poverty stereotyping and stigmatisation that shows little interest or regard for the truth. The reality is that very few benefit claimants have health issues of the sort described in these sensationalist stories. Chris Goulden from the JRF usefully reviewed the evidence on poverty and drug and alcohol addiction, and from the research concluded that 0.9% of adults are problem drug users and 3.8% are dependent on alcohol, with only 7% of people on benefits being problem drug users and 4% dependent on alcohol. Goulden concludes that

> The scales of the problems of poverty and addiction among parents are of different orders entirely. That's not to deny any link between the two: clearly poverty is a risk factor here, but there is much more to poverty than just addiction. Most people in poverty are not addicted to heroin, crack or alcohol but are just struggling to make ends meet. (Goulden, 2013)

Furthermore, as Alison Garnham, chief executive of the CPAG, has pointed out, 'Six in ten poor children have a parent who is a security guard or a cleaner rather than one who is a drug addict or "feckless"' (Garnham, 2012). Yet criminality and deviancy have long been staple issues in any discussion of poverty and the connection between the two is all too often assumed (Hancock and Mooney, 2013), in so far as there is either an implicit assumption or, more often than not these days, an explicit assertion by sections of the media and the political elite that

> Working class people, including those in receipt of welfare benefits, are frequently assumed to be more feckless, immoral and criminally-inclined than more affluent groups in popular discourse. (Hancock and Mooney, 2013, p 26)

In a review of the literature on poverty and crime for the JRF, Webster and Kingston point out that 'although the relationship between poverty and crime is not always direct, living in poverty makes offending and being a victim of crime much more likely' (Webster and Kingston, 2014, p 148). Yet, as Dorling has written, 'It could be argued that the most dangerous and frequent crimes in Britain are committed by the rich when they speed in their cars (which they often do)' (Dorling, 2014, p 2). Moreover, Hancock and Mooney point out that the 'actors with the most economic and political power routinely cause financial loss, harm and suffering on a much larger scale' (Hancock and Mooney, 2013, p 26). What might be more accurate to suggest is that certain types of crimes are more closely associated with people who experience poverty. Webster and Kingston have shown how acquisitive crime is strongly associated with unemployment and poverty. They also show how murder and violent crime, particularly that committed by and towards young men experiencing poverty, is directly correlated with experiences of deprivation and poverty (Webster and Kingston, 2014); and they point to the cumulative impacts of poverty more generally and how these may influence the chances of being involved in crime (as either a victim or a perpetrator). They point out that

> Long-term poverty adversely influences family functioning, engenders emotional stress and undermines emotional security, significantly increasing the risks of children beginning offending and continuing into teenage. (Webster and Kingston, 2014, p 148)

Gunter's research with young people in London has also illustrated how gang cultures thrive alongside wider issues in respect of the increasing poverty and marginalisation of young people in an otherwise affluent society (Gunter, 2017). These wider life conditions, experiences and events explain better than any inherent propensity or desire to be involved in crime why a minority of those in poverty are more likely to be involved in particular types of criminality. Indeed, as we will see through the remaining chapters of this book (especially in Chapter Three and Chapter Six), poverty itself thrusts people into risk-laden environments. In our research a small minority of young people did end up engaging in problematic drug use and, in some cases, in criminality. In our interviews with families experiencing deep and long-term poverty and whose lives were sometimes complexly 'troubled', a minority of our interviewees

> had become engaged in work in the criminal economy. Typically, this was in the form of acquisitive crime, such as shoplifting, or in drug dealing, both of which were often

motivated by a need to raise funds to support dependent drug use (e.g. of heroin or crack cocaine). Several people reported dealing or having dealt drugs (usually at the lower rungs of the local drug economy) ...//... The research neighbourhoods we studied had thriving drug markets. These individuals, leaving school unqualified and poorly educated, had found opportunities to work illegally in the drug trade to be more abundant and attractive than those in the formal economy. Some were engaged in drug dealing (and dependent drug use) before they even really contemplated searching for legal jobs. (Shildrick et al, 2012, pp 31 and 32)

Entrenched poverty limits opportunities and increases the risks that people face in their day-to-day lives. As we will see in the following chapters, for the vast majority this will not mean engaging in criminal activities. Moreover, empirical studies have shown how, while those living in deprived areas are often subjected to criminality in their neighbourhoods, those same neighbourhoods are also ones that people describe as offering safety and reassurance. The research participants in Lisa Mckenzie's study of St Anne's in Nottingham described how having close, supportive networks in and around the estates where they lived engendered a feeling of belonging and safety (Mckenzie, 2015). 'Being known' and 'knowing each other' helped people both in practical terms (like helping each other out with childcare or making sure children were safe) and in emotional terms, increasing a sense of connection and 'belonging' (Mckenzie, 2015, p 158). At the same time the obvious risks posed by high levels of crime on the estate were a source of concern and worry, particularly for mothers. As Mckenzie shows, violence and physical fighting are not altogether uncommon on poor estates, and while 'poor communities can be both a place of safety and a place where you can be valued' they can also be 'a pressure cooker filled with fear, anger, desperation and fragility' (Mckenzie, 2015, p 170). These complexities of home and neighbourhood were also apparent in our research projects. Interviewees valued their communities, neighbours and having family close by (which was often essential in helping people to get by on low incomes) but they also were often subjected to problems, such as exposure to crime, problematic drug dealing and use and, sometimes, personal victimisation (Shildrick et al, 2012a; 2012b).

From the respectable working class to the 'underclass'

Over the last 30 years or so poverty propaganda has flourished as working-class life conditions have been dramatically reshaped. Significant and lasting changes to working-class lives and opportunities have provided fertile ground for the stigma that lies at the heart of poverty propaganda to prosper. In recent years class – including what it means to be working class – has become more muddied (Savage, 2015), allowing those who are economically marginal (and generally working class, no matter which way you choose to measure it) to become vulnerable to stereotyping and stigmatisation. Poverty is increasingly associated with a 'left behind' set of people who reside somewhere on the margins.

Poverty propaganda works by seizing unusual events or moments of crisis to cement ideas of a group of undeserving, feckless people into the public imagination. The riots that took place in parts of Britain in 2011 were immediately grasped and utilised to ratchet up the volume of poverty propaganda (and pursue punitive criminal justice procedures on the back of it). Political figures were very quick to pass judgements on what had taken place. Kenneth Clarke, the then Justice Secretary, said, 'what I found most disturbing was the sense that the hard core of rioters came from a feral underclass' (Clarke, 2011), and David Cameron, the then Prime Minister, claimed that 'Pockets of our society are not just broken, but frankly they are sick' (Cameron, 2011). The notion that there are segments of society that are drifting away from the supposed mainstream, who experience poverty and a whole range of other social problems besides, is an important part of poverty propaganda. The popular daily tabloid the *Sun* ran a story that was not untypical, stressing the relationship between those involved in the riots and the 'welfare' system. It posited that 'THUGS held in the August riots were part of a feckless criminal underclass – with one in eight on DISABILITY benefits, figures revealed' (*Sun*, 24 October 2011). Of course, assuming that the figures were correct, the reality was that seven out of eight were *not* on disability benefits, but the facts are simply lost behind the inherent outrage that the comment is intended to provoke.

Neoliberalism dictates not just that segments of society are left behind, but that they, rather than the state, are responsible for their plight. The shifts in how class is understood and the confusion that surrounds what it means to be working class in Britain today have provided fertile ground for poverty propaganda to ensnare the working class in its net. This has been manufactured through narratives that stress that the left behind (or those who let themselves get left behind) form a recalcitrant underbelly of society. The 'troubled families' criminality narrative described above is frequently utilised to label the working class. As a consequence, the respectable – and largely respected – working class has much more routinely become an undesirable underclass. The underclass narratives are not new but they have been steadily reinforced and extended, to the point that the respectable working class is now much harder to locate, both literally and in the public's imagination.

Charles Murray, a US commentator turned amateur social scientist, played a key role in popularising this right-wing propaganda about poverty and its causes in the UK. His propositions about the supposed emergence of 'an underclass' (Murray, 1990) were influential, both because they played to themes that were already strongly apparent in the drift of political and policy commentary around poverty and worklessness (DWP, 2010; 2012) and because he was given significant space in the media to tout his ideas and make them accessible to a general audience. (The book returns to the question of how and why some ideas are given space in popular forums and others not in Chapter Seven.) Murray posited that he was interested not just in poverty, but in a 'type of poverty'. He argued that

> Britain has a growing population of work-aged, healthy people, who live in a different world from other Britons, who are raising their children to live in it, and whose values are now contaminating the values of entire neighbourhoods. (Murray, 1990, p 3)

It is important to recognise the importance of Murray's 'underclass' rhetoric in perpetuating myths about poverty in the contemporary context (see Welshman, 2006; MacDonald, 2007 for useful reviews of the idea of the underclass). In the event of the 2011 riots the concept of the underclass could be quickly seized upon and used to good effect because it already had a value in everyday language. Murray played a central role, supported and facilitated by a complicit media, in cementing the idea of people experiencing poverty who are deliberately deviant, work-shy and hence undeserving. Hence the notion that segments of our society are somehow out of step with the majority and subscribe to different values and behaviours is one that can usefully and readily be evoked and made use of at particular socio-economic and political moments. The riots paved the way for increased attention to the so-called 'troubled family' and for the doomed policy responses that are described above.

Social class has a particularly important place in poverty propaganda as well as in properly understanding poverty in the current social and political context (we discuss social class in more detail in Chapter Five). During the late 1950s and early 1960s 'being working class became fashionable' (Todd, 2014, p 236), but this is no longer the case. Reflecting on her own working-class origins, Mckenzie notes that 'I knew I was working class and I had been taught that we were the backbone of the country, strong and proud and it never occurred to me that "others" did not think the same' (Mckenzie, 2015, p 2). She writes that it was only in the 1980s that 'to be "working class" seemed old fashioned, silly and backward' (p 7). And it is hard to disagree with Todd when she argues that by the 1980s 'being working class had come to mean being poor, or living in fear of poverty' (Todd, 2014, p 336). To be working class is almost by default to be labelled as someone who is poor – not just economically lacking but culturally, personally and physically lacking too. Whole neighbourhoods or estates have been variously labelled as hotbeds of crime, of 'welfare dependency' and of despair (Hanley, 2012; Hancock and Mooney, 2013). These places are the supposed sanctuaries of the lazy, the work-shy and the generations of unemployed families all portrayed as happy enough in their hopelessness. These are the communities and people who are not just left behind but argued to be choosing to remain behind, complacent and content with their lot. Hanley points out that

> There is one phrase in the English language that has come
> to be larded with even more negative meaning than 'council
> estate' and that is 'tower block'...//... the word 'council'
> has become a pejorative term, which can be used to ridicule
> people's clothing, their hairstyles, their ways of speaking,
> the brands of cigarette they smoke and the alcohol they
> imbibe. (Hanley, 2012, p 97)

The Grenfell Tower fire disaster in the Borough of Kensington and Chelsea in London in June 2017 laid bare some of the dishonesty of this sort of poverty propaganda (as well as exposing many of the other inherent problems of neoliberal capitalism around safety and profits, social housing and power and responsibility, in addition to raising questions around whose voices matter). Quite who lived – and died – in Grenfell Tower is unlikely ever to be fully revealed, but what has become clear from the evidence to emerge so far is that the tower block housed a multitude of different sorts of people: working and retired; life-long Londoners, some of whom had lived in Grenfell for decades, along with those seeking sanctuary from war-torn places like Syria (see Shildrick, 2018, forthcoming). Yet negative class stereotyping tends to favour '"common sense" depictions of poverty' (Rogaly and Taylor, 2009, p 2) that revolve around stereotypes of '"white trash" and "chavs"' (Rogaly and Taylor, 2009, p 3) and that portray poor places and people in negative ways. Rogaly and Taylor go on to say that these sorts of labels are often used

> as shorthand simultaneously to describe and write off vast sections of Britain's population – often white, often living on council estates and nearly always poor. Such phrases deploy universalising stereotypes that link style and speech with educational aspirations, involvement with welfare and social control agencies and patterns of family behaviour. They also focus their spotlight solely on 'individuals', ridiculing or blaming them for their situation, and in so doing leave the context surrounding those individuals firmly out of the picture. (Rogaly and Taylor, 2009, p 3)

It is important to recognise that this generic negative stereotyping of the working class does much to power up poverty propaganda, extending its reach and furthering its stigma.

Conclusions

Holman points out that

> With almost boring repetitiveness vehement efforts have been exercised to impose a cleavage among the poor: those who are poor due to socio-economic and demographic factors outside their control; and those who are poor because of their own inadequate, deviant behaviour. It has been a common theme that this latter group of recalcitrant and wayward, pathological individuals and families constitutes a destabilising force. (Holman, 1994, p 143)

Lister (2004, p 100) recognises the importance of 'political struggles at the relational/symbolic rim of the poverty wheel as well as at its core'. As she notes, the poor are largely defined by the 'non-poor', whose discourses, attitudes and actions can have a profound impact on how poverty is experienced (Lister, 2004, p 100). Poverty as a condition and a concept has been lost behind a generic barrage of rhetoric around 'welfare dependency', undeservingness and any number of other social problems and issues. The power of these ideas, even as single concepts, can be immensely seductive, but as a collective their power is increased as they work to successfully cloud and crowd out the realities both of poverty as a condition and of what causes it. The notion that 'welfare' is problematic has widespread appeal, even to political figures on the supposed left of the political spectrum. Whether it is young mothers who are deemed to be 'milking the system' and choosing the 'mothering option' (Tyler, 2013; Jensen and Tyler, 2015) or simply the supposed work-shy layabouts who prefer benefits to work or live in families that have never had a job, the notion of the 'welfare scrounger' is cemented into the popular and public imagination. As we will see through the following pages of this book, not only is this a gross misrepresentation of the causes and consequences of poverty but it also directly paves the way for punitive policies that hurt those experiencing the condition and that serve to deepen inequalities of both outcomes and opportunities.

THREE

Poverty and lived experiences

Introduction

> Poverty is an outcome of severe economic stress and a lack of material goods ...//... the impact of poverty can bite deep into the home and family life, challenging parents' capacity to adequately provide for their children and creating the potential for stress, ill-health and in some cases discord. (Ridge, 2009, pp 25 and 30)

> "Get them [the government] to live on this street for four weeks ...//... they couldn't do it. They don't know what it's like to go to Netto coz they've never been. They haven't got a clue about the average person. They wouldn't know what it's like to pick something up and say I can't have that because I can't afford it or to say to your kids, 'you can't have that'." (Vera, 54-year-old Teesside interviewee in Shildrick et al, 2012b)

> "There are many complex reasons why people go to food banks." (Prime Minister Theresa May on *The Andrew Marr Show*, 30 April 2017)

The effects of poverty are material, physical and also increasingly recognised to be psychosocial (Walker and Chase, 2013; Walker, 2014; Mills, 2017). Yet poverty propaganda works to present those experiencing poverty – particularly those claiming out-of-work benefits – as living comfortably. The comparison between the ease and comfort of life on out-of-work benefits and the hardships of a life in paid work is frequently used to evoke prejudice towards 'welfare' claimants and engender feelings about unfairness in the system of social support. In the following chapter we will look at some of the difficulties of undertaking low-paid, insecure work and how this adds to the troubles of poverty, but in this chapter we look more closely at the experience of living with poverty and prioritise the accounts of people who have experienced the condition.

Close-up, qualitative, everyday accounts of poverty tend to be much more mundane than the popular and political narratives described in the previous chapter. Accounts of life from those who have experienced poverty also tend to be remarkably consistent. Research shows that those in poverty experience multiple hardships and disadvantages (Hooper et al, 2007; Ridge, 2009; Shildrick et al, 2012; Gordon et al, 2013; Shildrick and MacDonald, 2013; Cooper et al, 2014; Chase and Walker, 2015a, 2015b) and that resilience, fortitude and planning and negotiation are needed to manage day-to-day living on a low income. People rarely accept their situations with ease or anything remotely akin to joy as much poverty propaganda would have it, but often go to some lengths to try to mitigate poverty through seeking extra hours of work or getting into debt to meet essential immediate needs (Shildrick et al, 2012). Examples of the effects and experience of poverty appear throughout this book but this chapter gives space to the everyday experience of managing day-to-day living when experiencing poverty and its effects on health and well-being. The chapter also looks at the importance of 'welfare' reform in helping to understand the experience of poverty in the current context.

Struggling and getting by: the everyday experience of poverty

Living in poverty means that meeting daily basic needs is difficult, and sometimes well-nigh impossible. We see below how difficulties with the 'welfare' system and the increasing use of benefit sanctions have left people without any income at all, often for prolonged periods. Research consistently shows that living on a low income, for example out-of-work benefits, leaves people in financial hardship, and that people dealing with the effects of poverty suffer stress and guilt at being unable to meet their own and their children's basic needs (Shildrick et al, 2012a, 2012b; JRF, 2016). The anti-poverty strategy published by JRF in 2016 states that:

> Poverty means not being able to heat your home, pay your rent, or buy the essentials for your children. It means waking up every day facing insecurity, uncertainty, and impossible decisions about money. It means facing marginalization – and even discrimination – because of your financial circumstances. The constant stress it causes can overwhelm

people, affecting them emotionally and depriving them of the chance to play a full part in society. (JRF, 2016)

Yet research also shows that those who experience poverty are keen to demonstrate how they are able 'to cope' or 'to manage' – perhaps predictably, as a way of trying to maintain their dignity and self-respect and as a way of distancing themselves from the large and ever-expanding swathe of the supposedly 'undeserving poor' (Shildrick and MacDonald, 2013). Meeting everyday needs and managing on sometimes very low incomes involves effort and planning and 'sheer tenacity and determination just to keep going' (Bennett, 2008). Accessing simple necessary, everyday items, such as essential food items, has long been a struggle for those in poverty (Hooper et al, 2007; Bennett, 2008; Shildrick et al, 2012; Patrick, 2017), but as poverty increases and many ordinary people see their incomes decline, these problems are inevitably amplified and extended. A report in 2014 found that

> People on low incomes have traded down and down again to the cheapest products, after which they simply have to buy less food. We have spoken to people living on one meal a day, drinking hot water and lemon to tame hunger pangs, trying to think how they can survive on a budget of £6 a week. More than half a million children are now living in families who are unable to provide a minimally acceptable diet. (Cooper et al, 2014, p 4)

Patrick's research has demonstrated the ways in which food has to be tightly rationed over days so as to eke out at least something to eat each day (Patrick, 2017). In my own research projects respondents reported very similar experiences. They frequently described having to plan meals carefully and try to make them last over a number of days. This process of making food last or other strategies such as relying on family members to provide a cooked meal was a necessity (Shildrick et al, 2012a). As in other research, our interviewees regularly described 'bulking out' meals, using rice as a cheap way to try to make meals more filling, or living on eggs or soup (Shildrick et al, 2012a). It was also commonplace to time visits to the shops so as to get reduced-price fresh items such as bread and eggs. These were all practices that were born of necessity rather than thrift, and also had implications for daily routines and reduced flexibility, particularly for those with childcare responsibilities or who did not live close to large supermarkets. Parents, and most frequently mothers, experiencing poverty often miss meals in order to provide for their children (Ridge, 2002; Young Women's Trust, 2017). Loopstra and Lalor (2017) report that respondents in their research into food bank usage 'were cutting back on food intake, experiencing hunger and/or going whole days without eating because they lacked enough money for food' (p x). For those in poverty the 'going without' in order to protect children, the practice of 'robbing Peter to pay Paul' as debts mount up, amounts to little more than the normalisation of 'everyday hardship' (Chase and Walker, 2015b, p 162). Hence, 'In the current era of austerity, with high costs of living, stagnating incomes, and rising levels of inequality the question of how well all people are able to eat is increasingly urgent' (Lambie-Mumford and O'Connell, 2015, p 1). One of the key implications of managing on a low income is reduction of choice, and this plays out across all aspects of life, limiting both material comforts and life chances and opportunities. These issues will be picked up in Chapter Five, where we learn how poverty is related to class inequalities and the reproduction of life chances. Chase and Walker (2015b) point out that the people experiencing poverty in their research 'described regularly facing difficult decisions over whether to pay bills or provide food and clothing for children' (p 162). They argue that

> The constant daily challenges of running a home and supporting a family were frequently denoted by phrases such as 'struggling', 'nightmare', 'going round and round in circles', 'struggling to keep head above water', 'scuppered', 'stuck in a rut', 'scrimp, save, borrow, beg and steal', 'robbing Peter to pay Paul', 'battering your head against the wall'. (Chase and Walker, 2015b, p 162)

Indeed, finding and keeping a home at all is another area of difficulty for people experiencing poverty. Tunstall et al (2013) have shown how housing costs can be a factor that pushes people into poverty, but more prevalent is the problem that poverty impacts on people's housing options. Too often, people experiencing poverty have limited housing options and are more likely to be forced to live in damp, overcrowded or simply unsuitable properties. Poverty also renders people more at risk of eviction and homelessness and this is a problem that has escalated as a result of 'welfare' reforms. At the time of writing, just as Universal Credit was about to be rolled out across the country it was widely reported that in the areas where the system had been piloted rent arrears and homelessness had rocketed (Savage and Jayanetti, 2017). The impact of 'welfare' reform on those experiencing poverty is discussed further below, but in respect of the impact of Universal Credit it has been suggested by the parliamentary enquiry looking at its roll-out that

> The Department for Work and Pensions evaluation found that 42% of all claimant families surveyed said the wait for a first universal credit payment to be processed and DWP [Department for Work and Pensions] administrative errors were the cause of their rent arrears. Four in 10 households were in rent arrears eight weeks after the claim was made, with nearly one in three still in arrears four months later. One in five owed £1,000 or more. Four out of five said they had never been in arrears before. (Butler, 2017)

Watt has looked at the London housing market, where housing has become a critical site of class struggle, and argues that social housing has moved from a situation whereby it catered 'for large tranches of the population', namely 'the industrial working class', to its more frequent depiction today as '"sink estates" – stigmatized urban poverty, misery and lawlessness' (Watt, 2017, pp 2–3) that were deemed to lack 'effective role models and connections to the world of work' (Watt, 2017, p 4). As Watt acknowledges, the residents of social housing often view their homes very positively, but pressures on social housing have meant that, particularly in places like London, social housing tenants have been subjected to brutal treatment, involving displacement to towns and cities they neither know nor wish to live in. Watt and Minton (2016) argue that 'London's struggling multi-ethnic, working classes have been lingering in the Godotesque queue for social housing for many years' (p 204) but recent cuts to 'welfare' have resulted in what many have described as 'social cleansing' (Watt and Minton, 2016, p 201) as London councils export their homeless families into temporary accommodation in cheaper areas either within or outside London. In July–September 2015 one third (17,120) of London's 50,490 households living in temporary accommodation were located in another local authority (Watt and Minton, 2016, p 204).

Not being able to heat one's home properly is an important feature of life on a low income (Shildrick et al, 2010; Daly and Kelly, 2015). Rising heating costs have resulted in widespread fuel poverty, and not just for those living in poverty. Hills (2012) declared fuel poverty to be 'a serious national problem' (p 4) and one that without doubt 'compounds the problem of poverty' (p 2). Research with those experiencing poverty reports the ways in which they work to cope when they cannot afford to heat their homes as and when they really need to. A respondent in Daly and Kelly's research puts it like this, "I would rather sit with a jumper on when the kids are at school than turn my heating on 'coz that's wasting it. It's different if the kids are in. I need it on then. But me and him can put jumpers on and layer up" (Daly and Kelly, 2015). Similar stories emanated from my own research on numerous occasions. Janice, a respondent in one of our studies, described the problem of heating her home:

Janice:	I mean we can't afford to get the heating done and that's not ideal, especially with me getting chest infections – but we can't do anything about it. You just have to get on with it, keep going sort of thing. Heating broke five weeks ago and we can't afford to have it fixed.
Interviewer:	So how's it been for you, how have you managed?
Janice:	Cold! [*laughs*] There's no heating, there's no hot water …
Lennie:	We've been sleeping down here … we listen to the weather forecast and because the past couple of nights it was due to plummet, so we stayed down here because up there it's freezing cold …
Janice:	It's bitter cold … you can't even go in the bath to get warmed up because there's no hot water. There's the shower but you're that bloody cold when you get out. So I go to me daughter's next door but one for a bath … my bones ache, don't they? Really ache. I just cannot get warm. He puts that on full [*points to electric heater*] but I still cannot get warm, so it's pointless wasting the gas. (Shildrick et al, 2010, p 35)

Research for the Institute for Fiscal Studies (IFS) reported that 'cold weather shocks translate into adverse income shocks' (Beatty et al, 2011, p 3) and that the effects are worst for the 'poorest households' (p 17). It concluded that for some households there are significant reductions in food spending, resulting in a 'heat or eat' trade-off. In our research one mother reported how she resorted to "playing dinosaurs" (hiding with the children under the duvets) to keep warm (Shildrick et al, 2012a).

Unsurprisingly, debt features strongly in the lives of those experiencing poverty, as research shows that the 'poverty premium' is a further drain on limited economic resources. Debt is most often fuelled by the demands of daily life and the inability to manage day-to-day expenses and necessities. Hartfree and Collard (2014) point out that 'some of the characteristics of households with problem debt are the same characteristics associated with households in poverty, reflecting the link between problem debt and low income' (p 7). They conclude that there is 'clear evidence that low-income households are more likely to experience problem debt than higher income households' (p 11). Moreover,

> Whilst for some households in the longitudinal qualitative research problem debt started as a result of a single specific event, such as losing a job or starting a family, for others it resulted from a sequence of events or accumulation of adverse circumstances over a period of time, with no single trigger or cause. Low income was an underlying cause whereby household finances were precarious and easily susceptible to disruption by a fall in income or an increase in demands on expenditure that, in the absence of savings or other resources to draw on, led households to using credit and defaulting on payments. (Hartfree and Collard, 2014, p 11)

Because they are often unable to access mainstream lenders or sources of credit, those on low incomes tend to be forced to use higher-cost credit. This means that they are more likely to use pay-day lenders and pawnbrokers, who charge significantly more for borrowing. The use of this form of credit also tends to be cumulative, in that collectors come to the door and treat customers more like friends, lulling them into a false sense of security and selling them further credit when they are unable to pay off original loans – thus serving to alleviate suffering in the short term but deepening disadvantage over the longer term. I witnessed these encounters myself during the course of some of my fieldwork and on one occasion I gave an interviewee the money we paid people for participating in the research (£20) to help her appease a persistent doorstep loan collector who had called at her home mid-way through our interview. It is widely accepted that those experiencing poverty also pay more – commonly referred to as a 'poverty premium' – for everyday essential services. The term was first conceived in the US and refers to the ways in which those experiencing poverty pay more for household fuel, telecommunications, insurance, food and grocery shopping, access to money and the higher cost of credit (Davies et al, 2016). Save the Children (2007) reported that

It is a shocking injustice that the poorest families in the UK pay higher prices than better-off families for basic necessities like gas, electricity and banking. The costs that poor families bear in acquiring cash and credit, and in purchasing goods and services, can amount to a 'poverty premium' of around £1,000 – 9 per cent of the disposable income of an average-size family. (Save the Children, 2007, p 1)

As Schmuecker (2017) argues, the 'poverty premium' costs low-income households on average £490 a year. The pressures and practical difficulties of managing on a low income have emotional as well as physical implications. Dawn, a woman interviewed in research by Strelitz and Lister (2008), described the pressures she felt:

"My second son, Tom, has got special needs. I am under pressure. They are looking for the latest jeans and I do get under pressure because I can't afford them. I would love to be able to put the kids in more clubs and for them to join things, but at the present time I can't do it. I try to bring them to the park and do things, you know, and they are looking for football kits and things like that, but I just can't do it." (Strelitz and Lister, 2008, p 7)

Dawn talks about how her children are entitled to free school meals because of their low income but refuse to take them because they feel 'embarrassed'. She points out that children who collect a school lunch provided by the school are bullied by other children (p 10). Children living in families experiencing poverty frequently report being embarrassed that their parents cannot afford meals and by the systems used in schools that still, in some cases, administer free meals in a way that makes those in receipt of them readily identifiable, and thus at risk of being bullied and stigmatised (Holloway et al, 2014). Some children report missing meals altogether so as to avoid this situation (Holloway et al, 2014). Children brought up in poverty are not immune to the pressures that their parents face, and research shows that they too feel anxiety and often work hard to try and protect their parents (Ridge, 2002). Children in poverty report that they all too often feel 'singled out, stigmatized and bullied' (Holloway et al, 2014, p 8).

As is pretty obvious from the discussion above, many of the problems and difficulties associated with poverty are interconnected. As Beck (2002) argues 'poverty attracts an unfortunate abundance of risks'. Hence it is not difficult to understand how the effects are also cumulative. Alice was a participant in a study by Zipfel and colleagues and her story typifies how the problems of poverty can build up over time, weakening health and worsening life chances:

> Alice lives with her son aged five, and daughter aged eight. They have a three bedroomed council house. Alice isn't in paid employment and they receive no support from the children's fathers. She has no formal qualifications but 'would like to work with children'. She has difficulty reading and writing. She has intimated that she might be pregnant. Alice feels harassed by Job Centre Plus. She was 'just about' coping two or three years ago but is now increasingly in debt, is stressed and suffers from mental health problems. She is devoted to her children but her life is now dominated by worries about providing them with food and other essentials. Christmas and birthdays are a particular time of dread. (Zipfel et al, 2015, p 17)

Alice's story is very typical of accounts of how the problems of experiencing poverty can quickly escalate and accumulate. One problem can often lead to another or be piled on top of other existing problems, leading to greater difficulties in resisting or managing the condition (Shildrick et al, 2012; Daly and Kelly, 2015; Zipfel et al, 2015).

The nature of life lived in conditions of poverty has implications for escape from poverty and for prospects of social mobility, as we will learn in Chapter Five. What this section has illustrated is the ways in which experiencing poverty impacts heavily and negatively on people's ability to meet basic and everyday needs. This is in stark contrast to some of the popular and political accounts of what it is like to live in poverty. Research consistently shows that those experiencing poverty encounter significant hardship in simply trying to survive from day to day and meet very basic needs in respect of food, clothing and housing.

Ill health and poverty

As Peter Townsend noted, 'whatever we may mean by poverty, there are people whose resources are so low that they bear the observable and objective marks of multiple deprivation, including ill-health or disability and the risk of early death' (Townsend, 1979, p 125). It has long been recognised that stark inequalities in health exist between different social classes and that those experiencing poverty and other associated disadvantages tend also to experience poorer health. Graham points out that

> Social class is 'written on the body'. It is inscribed in our experiences of health and our chances of premature death. The invariable pattern, across time and between societies, is one in which men and women in higher socio-economic groups enjoy better health across longer lives than those in lower socio-economic groups. These inequalities in health are persisting – and in some cases widening – in the context of rapid economic and social change in the UK. (Graham, 2006, p 240)

Across all dimensions of health, those experiencing poverty have poorer outcomes. Dorling (2016) argues that 'inequality kills, slowly, gently, just a small additional effect every day' (p xii) because it leads to a greater likelihood of physical and mental ill health, disability and early death.

As part of our low pay, no pay study (Shildrick et al, 2012a) I interviewed Roy (aged 50) and his daughter Carol (aged 26) in 2011 (Shildrick et al, 2012b). Their example illustrates the complexity that ill health can add to families' experiences of poverty and their ability to engage in paid employment. Roy had been unable to work because of health issues since his early 20s and faced serious and life-limiting health difficulties. His wife was his carer. Carol, Roy's daughter, had two children (aged 4 and 7) and had never had a paid job. She had left school at 16 with some qualifications and completed a childcare course at college. At age 17 she had started another college course, in performing arts, but had dropped out half way through. Carol had her first child at 20, and she talked about having wanted to be a mother from a very early age. Carol was volunteering four days a week and aimed eventually to get a paid job working with children. Roy and his wife had other children (now adults) who also had life-limiting disabilities, but they were a close-knit family and visited each other daily, living just streets apart. Their health conditions placed significant challenges on them all, both as individuals and in respect of their responsibilities to each other. The caring demands were borne largely by the family – at significant savings to the state – but their health-related conditions had implications for their ability to engage in paid employment (Shildrick et al, 2012b). Another family in our research talked of the additional financial strain of travelling up to Newcastle and coping with a seriously ill child, which had led to one parent having to leave a low-paid job (that typically did not afford compassionate leave for family difficulties), and which had imposed significant additional strain on their lives on top of the stress of having a seriously ill child (Shildrick et al, 2012a). The lived experiences of ill health among people experiencing poverty and related disadvantages often reveal not just a significant volume of adverse health events and conditions but the challenge of facing ill health, and in some cases multiple bereavements, on a very low income (Shildrick et al, 2012a).

Bambra (2016) has shown how these inequalities also have a geographical dimension, with people living in the North of England having consistently poorer health than those in the South. Bambra and colleagues' work has highlighted the ways in which the health of people living in some of the older industrial regions suffers the penalties of both geography and class. Bambra (2016) has pointed out how the 'English health divide is the largest in Europe' (p 11). She posits that 'It is not universally "grim up North" or "pleasant down South". These patterns arise because the North–South health divide is supplemented by a second, more widespread divide in health between regions and within towns and cities – a divide between affluent and deprived areas' (Bambra, 2016, p 17). These geographical divides of inequality and poverty will be explored further in Chapter Five, where the role of labour markets in producing and perpetuating poverty will be explored in more detail.

As well as physical health effects, poverty takes its toll on people's psychological well-being. Issues of stigma and shame are particularly important, as discourses that depict the poor as 'other' label those in poverty as being to blame for their position (Bos et al, 2013; Chase and Walker, 2013; Fell and Hewstone, 2015). Mental ill health is strongly associated with poverty. As Fell and Hewstone argue, 'poverty increases the risk of mental illness, including schizophrenia, depression, anxiety and substance addiction. Poverty can act as a causal factor and as a consequence' (Fell and Hewstone, 2015, p 1). Evidence is emerging that since the recession of 2008 that there has been an increasing incidence of ill health and suicides. Evidence from Greece has shown dramatic rises in the numbers of people committing suicide since the onset of the economic crisis (Harrison, 2015). In the UK recent research also suggests that there has been a significant increase in suicides since the onset of austerity, particularly among men. Barnes et al (2016) argue that the recession was 'associated with a reversal of previously falling suicide rates in England as well as increases in suicide attempts and depression' (p 1). They note that this is 'only the tip of the iceberg' (p 2), with much more going unreported, and write that 'Unemployment, financial difficulties, debt and loss of a home increase an individual's risk of depression, suicide attempt and suicide' (p 2). This issue has also been highlighted in research by Mills, who has shown that

> Since the financial recession and subsequent austerity driven welfare reform, increasing numbers of people in receipt of benefits in the UK are committing suicide. Media coverage of individual suicides, along with public domain suicide notes, and letters from coroners to the Department for Work and Pensions, have been amassed by anti-cuts and disabled people's organizations to create public archives of 'austerity suicides' and 'welfare reform deaths'. (Mills, 2017, p 1)

'Welfare' reform has been heavily criticised for the increase in suicides and deaths. The DWP came under increased pressure to release figures showing how many people had died under the process of 'welfare' reform. Eventually figures were released, over a bank holiday weekend in August 2015. The department pointed out that no 'causal effects' (DWP, 2015) could be assumed. The DWP and the Secretary of State, Iain Duncan Smith, tried to limit the damage of these statistics and to fudge their meaning, hoping that their official pronouncements would trash the numerous qualitative personal accounts of 'welfare' reform that reveal the sheer brutality of the bureaucracy being wrought on people who are already sick and vulnerable. Some of these cases have been relatively widely published on social media – for example, the case of David Clapson, who died as the result of a diabetic coma and who was found to have had no food in his stomach at the time of his death. Mr Clapson had been sanctioned and had lost his benefits because he had missed a meeting at the Job Centre. He was a diabetic and he needed money to pay for electricity for his fridge, where he needed to keep his insulin. He could afford neither electricity nor food. It was widely reported that he was found with a pile of CVs next to his body (Ryan, 2014). A series of internal inquiries into the deaths of people claiming 'welfare' were finally released in response to Freedom of Information requests (Butler and Pring, 2016). Butler and Pring (2016) conclude that:

> A series of secret internal inquiries into the deaths of people claiming social security reveal that ministers were repeatedly warned of shortcomings in the treatment of vulnerable claimants facing potentially traumatic cuts to their benefits entitlements.

Many cases have been brought to light, particularly via activists and on social media. For example, in 2014 a coroner's office sent a 'Prevention of future deaths report' to the DWP (Judiciary, 2014) outlining concerns about a suicide case in which, the coroner believed, the suicide had been triggered by the subject's (a Mr Sullivan) recent assessment as fit for work. Mr Sullivan had been found to be 'fit for work' despite the fact that he very clearly was not 'fit for work' and that his own GP had assessed him as not being fit for work. He had been declared to be fit by someone who (according to the coroner's report) was not medically trained. These are not isolated cases, and even if they were they represent an appalling and unnecessary level of suffering, and all as a direct consequence of inept government attempts to cut 'welfare' spending. Recent research (Barr et al, 2015) has shown that the ways in which 'welfare' reforms are being implemented are associated with adverse effects on mental health. Barr and colleagues conclude that

> The programme of assessing people on disability benefits, using the Work Capability Assessment, was independently associated with an increase in suicides, self-reported mental health problems and anti-depressant prescribing. The policy may have had serious adverse consequences for mental health in England which could outweigh any benefits that arise from moving people off disability benefits. (Barr et al, 2015, p 1)

This chapter now turns to the impacts of 'welfare' reform on those experiencing poverty, and particularly those who are reliant on out-of-work benefits.

Poverty, austerity and 'welfare' reform

The central plank of the austerity measures that have been put in place since 2010 has been to cut public spending, and while these measures, particularly in respect of 'welfare' reform, have been implemented by the recent Coalition and Conservative administrations, they have also drawn support from many who reside more towards the political Left. A good part of the explanation for this is the success of poverty propaganda, and I will return to this issue in Chapter Seven. Duffy has shown how the cuts have placed an unfair burden on the poorest in society, with disabled people being particularly adversely affected (Duffy, 2013). Around 70% of the cuts fall in four main areas: English local government, benefits, universities and criminal justice. Together, local government cuts and the 'welfare' cuts make up the significant majority. These latter two budgets have a strong remit to cater for those experiencing poverty and disadvantage and they aim to help meet basic needs among groups who are in most need of support. There have been multiple changes to the 'welfare' system. They have impacted the most on those on the lowest incomes and this has all taken place amid a hostile labour market (see Chapter Four) and cuts to public services.

Writing of the uneven impact of recent 'welfare' reforms, Beatty and Fothergill (2016) argue that the reforms 'hit the poorest places hardest because they generally have large numbers of people reliant on benefits', but note also that 'the reforms extend well beyond just those who are out of work to include significant swathes of the employed population as well' (p 5). It is becoming clear that many of the changes to out-of-work benefits are impacting on the same families, who were previously in receipt of several different 'benefits', meaning that some families have been faced with a 'perfect storm' of assaults on their ability to secure a decent standard of living (Oxfam, 2012, p 1) at a time when many were already struggling to make ends meet.

Of particular concern here is the issue of 'welfare' conditionality that has largely been brought to bear because of the success of the sorts of poverty propaganda discussed in this book. Under recent changes to 'welfare' provision, claimants have been subjected to greater and ever more stringent rules and regulations in order to claim any payments, particularly in respect of out-of-work benefits. It has been argued that these changes have constituted the biggest and most radical changes to social security since the inception of the welfare state. The idea of sanctions in the benefits system is not new. 'Welfare' policy in the UK since the turn of the century has moved to a system of 'workfare' that is characterised by increased conditionality. Prior to the general election of May 2015, Beatty et al (2015, p 2) argued that

> Conditionality backed by sanctions, has been a feature of the British social security system since the late 1980s but intensified with the introduction of JSA in 1996 and the New Labour Governments of 1997–2010 which placed conditionality at the heart of their welfare reforms. This approach was advanced further by the present Coalition Government which is in the process of implementing the harshest regime of conditionality in the history of the British benefit system.

The New Labour approach placed 'conditionality and responsibility at the heart of welfare policy' (Beatty et al, 2015, p iv), but the Coalition government escalated the policy and embedded it in a wider process of 'welfare' reform that sees 'welfare' claimants having their benefits reduced. Sanctions were introduced because, it is argued, they 'promote more active job search, deter voluntary unemployment and encourage entry into the labour market by those who have not previously been required to show they were available for work' (Manchester Citizens Advice, 2013, p 4). The notion of sanctioning people for not complying with what is required of them in terms of job search, and as a way of supposedly encouraging people into work, fits neatly with the prevailing political and public consensus on 'welfare'. Three grades or categories of sanctions have been introduced that are argued to correlate with the seriousness of the 'offence'. Thus, a third 'offence' sanction can be applied for a period of up to three years. While the sticks applied to benefit claimants have been increased, the 'Claimant Commitment' was also introduced to set out more clearly the expectations on benefit claimants, who are now expected to fulfil a greater number of activities in order to claim benefits. Moreover, specific targets, for example in respect of the number of jobs that claimants are expected to apply for, and required attendance at meetings with advisors, were introduced. Failure to comply with these often onerous demands results in sanctions being applied. Claimants who are sanctioned are eligible to apply for hardship payments, although if they have no children they will not receive any such payments (assuming their claim is successful) for at least 14 days. Evidence is emerging that benefit claimants who are sanctioned are rarely advised about claiming these payments (Church Action on Poverty, 2015), are left destitute and are frequently sanctioned for onerous reasons or for incredibly minor infringements. Dwyer and colleagues are working on the biggest and most ambitious research project on conditionality to be undertaken so far (see www. welfareconditionality.ac.uk). Dwyer and Wright (2014, p 30) argue in respect of the move towards a more punitive system that

> This formulation is problematic in several respects, not least because it holds individuals as primarily responsible for the adverse life situations they experience, without regard for: personal impairments and health-related needs; broader structural causes of unemployment (such as the global economic crisis which has led to recession and prolonged economic downturn causing redundancies and constrained labour market opportunities); and responsibilities to others,

such as the care needs of family members. The tone of reforms has also been shaped by powerful stigmatising anti-welfare rhetoric and a well-established and on-going priority of cost cutting.

The coalition of churches has argued that 'Sanctions are more than a simple withholding of benefit whilst a person is not compliant, they are imposed for fixed periods, effectively making them a deliberate punishment' (Church Action on Poverty et al, 2015, p 3). There is debate over how many sanctions have been applied. The DWP counts each benefit separately and in August 2017 reported that 2.1 million decisions had been made to apply some sort of sanction to claimants of JSA alone (DWP, 2017). Webster has been highly critical of the whole system of sanctions. Collecting systematic evidence of the application of benefit sanctions over a period of six years, he suggests that the system is 'out of control' and 'heaping more pressure on claimants than any policy since the abolition of the workhouse' (Webster, 2017). In September 2017 he reported that:

> In the year to March 2017 there were approximately 129,000 JSA and 229,000 UC [Universal Credit] sanctions on unemployed people before challenges, a total of 358,000. This is an increase over the revised figure of 328,000 for calendar 2016. Over the period August 2015 to March 2017, the rate of UC sanctions was 7.4% of claimants per month. This is three times the rate of 2.5% for JSA. It makes the overall rate 3.8% for JSA and UC combined. Because of DWP backlogs, at present it is impossible to say whether there is a trend in the UC sanction rate, but the overall rate of sanction on unemployed people is likely to rise simply because of the continuing transfer of claimants to the high-sanctioning UC. The UC sanction rate is higher than JSA for every age group, by amounts varying from 58% to 122%.

The United Nations Committee on the Rights of Persons with Disabilities has expressed concern about the impact of sanctions, particularly for those claimants with disabilities. As Webster (2017) correctly points out, the Committee's report (United Nations, 2017) is incredibly difficult to locate but very clearly states that the government is failing to meet its obligations under the UN Convention on the Rights of Persons with Disabilities. The report expresses concern about the 'the detrimental impact of the Employment and Support

Allowance conditionality and sanctions on persons with disabilities' (United Nations, 2017, p 14) and calls for the government to tackle the negative consequences on the mental health and situation of persons with disabilities (United Nations, 2017, p 15).

Even before this dramatic increase in the use of sanctions there was much evidence to show that claimants of out-of-work benefits not only intensely dislike having to claim any sort of 'welfare' but often find encounters with organisations such as Jobcentre Plus not just humiliating but difficult to navigate. The fraught and stressful nature of these encounters was something that Kayleigh Garthwaite and I witnessed many times in our numerous days spent hanging around in Jobcentre Plus attempting to recruit people for our studies. Claimants are often confused about decisions that are made about their claims and are often left struggling to understand why payments might be delayed (Shildrick et al, 2012a). In respect of sanctions much evidence is emerging that many people are left completely in the dark about why they have had their benefits withdrawn (Manchester Citizens Advice, 2013; Webster, 2017). Evidence is also mounting that sanctions increasingly leave people destitute and vulnerable to homelessness. A report in 2015 showed that where people had been sanctioned 21% reported that they had become homeless as a result of the sanctions and nearly eight out of ten had gone hungry or skipped meals (Beatty et al, 2015). As Dwyer and Wright (2014) point out:

> The scope and significance of this new system of standardised welfare conditionality is unprecedented in offloading the welfare responsibilities of the state and employers onto citizens who are in receipt of *in work* and *out of work* social security benefits. Unemployed and low paid citizens are now held to be solely responsible, not only for a lack of paid employment, but also partial engagement with the paid labour market and the levels of remuneration they may receive. (p 33)

Jobcentre Plus workers have talked about the absurdity and cruelty in the system that they are required to administer. One such adviser, interviewed by O'Hara, talked of the 'quagmire that awaits people caught in the welfare system' (O'Hara, 2015b). The same adviser talked of many wrong decisions being imposed and said that advisers often felt they were being stripped of the power to help clients. She went on to point out:

"You are not doing the job. You're fire fighting. From my own experience staff are subject to constant and aggressive pressure to meet and exceed targets. Colleagues would leave team meetings crying. Advisors were actively encouraged to apply sanctions to contribute to the points system that ranks job centre offices. It was often for stupid reasons. A customer would maybe be a bit late, or would phone in and the message wasn't passed on. It was very distressing to have customers literally without food, without heat, without resources and these were unwell and disabled customers." (Cited in O'Hara, 2015b)

One of the key arguments for sanctions is that they are intended to focus people's minds more firmly on job searching, yet Arni et al (2013) argue that the application of benefit sanctions lowers the quality of subsequent jobs for job seekers who have been sanctioned. This is the case in terms of both job duration and earnings. Perhaps unsurprisingly, evidence also shows that rather than helping to shift job seekers closer to the labour market the application of sanctions serves to shift focus away from job searching. Research by Herden and colleagues has shown how the imposition of sanctions throws people's lives into chaos and pushes job searching to the back as people turn to dealing with the immediate demands of trying to survive (Herden et al, 2015). Furthermore, they conclude that 'Sanctions cause debt and increase household vulnerability and decrease job seekers' capacity to go out into the jobs market' (Herden et al, 2015, p 6). In the chapter that follows we learn more about the relationship between paid work and poverty, but it should hardly be rocket science to realise that depriving people who are already trying to navigate life on a low income – and all of the challenges and difficulties that this inevitably entails – will only serve to make a bad situation worse and, for many, make entry into employment less, not more likely. Even where people are moved towards paid work on the back of losing their benefit payments, there are serious questions to be asked about the nature and quality of that employment (Webster, 2017) and whether such employment will take the person or family away from poverty (Shildrick et al, 2012a), over and above the impact on personal health and well-being.

If the aim of sanctions is to punish people and cause immense suffering, then some may perceive the regime a success, but there are 'systematic flaws' in the way sanctions are being imposed. Sanctions all too often leave people who are already experiencing poverty completely destitute, which has longer-term implications for people's lives, as well as immediate impacts on their ability to survive, let alone search for and find a job. Sanctions have little or no effect in moving people towards work and, perversely, but perhaps not surprisingly, undermine people's ability to focus on job search and diminish their future job prospects. Quite simply, benefit sanctions are cruel, ineffective and not fit for purpose. In 2016 the United Nations expressed 'serious concern' about levels of inequality in the UK and declared that the 'UK government's austerity measures and social security reforms are in breach of their obligations to human rights' (UN Economic and Social Council, Committee on Economic and Social Rights, 2016). Yet the report passed by with barely a mention, drowned out completely by the ever-growing and deafening volume of poverty propaganda.

Food bank Britain

The pressure to make the right, healthy eating choices has become an integral aspect of neoliberal Britain, where individuals are expected to take responsibility for eating healthily. It is often mothers who have practical day-to-day responsibility for providing meals for children, and increasingly it is mothers who are tasked with the responsibility of providing not just any food but those foods that are deemed appropriate and healthy. As Pike and Kelly (2014) argue, food has come to symbolise 'a complex set of consumer practices' that encompass moral and ethical dimensions as much as physical (p xiv). Certain foods such as 'burgers and ready meals' provoke ready judgements about the 'sorts of people' who might eat them (Pike and Kelly, 2014, p xi). Cheaper foods are both a necessity and a source of stigma and shame. For Crossley (2017) 'the imagery of poor families eating takeaway food in front of the television is part of a wider narrative about the alleged poor dietary habits and culinary skills among working class families' (p 89).

In our research food emerged as a site for stigma and shame: mothers talked negatively about other mothers who filled their supermarket trollies with cheap foods that were deemed to be inappropriate and unhealthy (see Shildrick and MacDonald, 2013). Lady Jenkins' comments, quoted in the Introduction, on the value of porridge over sugary cereal, and her explicit assertion that those experiencing poverty would be more likely to choose the latter, plays to a dominant class-shaming narrative that has widespread resonance and appeal. Food shame and shaming is only a part of the much more widely spread poverty stigma (see Chapter Six for a fuller discussion of poverty, stigma and shame). Yet what these depictions and narratives hide is the very real challenges that face families in respect of meeting one of the most fundamental aspects of human need.

One very visible aspect of the abundance of food poverty has been the dramatic rise in the existence and use of food banks over recent years. In fact, it is this issue that has forced at least some open discussion of poverty back onto the public and political agenda. The main reason why the proliferation of food banks has provoked debate is that they are a visible face of poverty and many people have, quite rightly, questioned why such a seemingly desperate measure should be needed in a rich country such as the UK. Of course, much of the popular and political discussion has focused on individual and pathologising explanations for the existence of food banks. Chris Steward, a Conservative city councillor, said that living standards had surged, there was no need for food banks, they were an insult to starving people around the world and donating to them allowed recipients to spend more money on alcohol and cigarettes (Aitchison, 2013). Michael Gove MP continued this popular rhetoric by arguing that the inability of those experiencing poverty to manage their money was the driving force behind food banks. Just as with Jacob Rees-Mogg MP, cited in the Introduction, these pronouncements might seem lazy or simply reflective of individual ignorance, but in fact they are more cleverly orchestrated and manufactured to deliberately obfuscate and muddy the waters and play into and perpetuate poverty propaganda. The real reasons for the explosion in the existence and necessity of food banks – and the dire consequences that would ensure for many if they didn't exist – can remain hidden. So, when scientists and public health doctors warn of a 'public health emergency' as malnutrition cases increase amid austerity measures (Ashton et al, 2014) , the government continues to insist that benefits are set at a level such that people 'can afford to eat' and that food banks are only really aimed at helping where people might 'have short-term shortages or where they feel they need a bit of extra food' (Jowit, 2013).

However, food banks or emergency food provision are not new, and in various forms they have long featured in the UK and other parts of the world. What has changed relatively recently is that they have become much more prevalent and they have also, for many, become a mainstream aspect of 'welfare' provision. As Riches (2002) points out, 'in the last twenty years food banks have established themselves as one of the fastest growing charitable industries in first world societies' (p 648). Reporting on the rise of food banks in Canada, Riches argues that they represent the 'breakdown of Canada's social safety net' (p 658). Since the austerity agenda was brought to the fore in the

UK under the Coalition government that came to power in 2010, and which has continued under the Conservative administration in office at the time of writing, the use of food banks in the UK has increased five-fold, a development that many people attribute to the impact of 'welfare' reform (Morse, 2013). As Riches (2002) points out, in the early 2000s food banks were in their 'infancy' in the UK, but they came to prominence under the Coalition government on account of their rapid increase in numbers. The Trussell Trust, the main official food bank provider in the UK, has expanded rapidly over recent years. Evidence shows that delays in paying benefit claims are a key reason for people's being referred to food banks, although evidence is now also emerging that 'working families are increasingly having to turn to food banks and credit to make ends meet' (Sentamu et al, 2014, p 6). Garthwaite's ethnographic work in food banks in the North-East of England shows how many food bank users are already struggling with health conditions, some of which require special attention to what they can and cannot eat. She reports (in line with other evidence) that there is a high rate of mental illness, particularly depression and anxiety, among food bank users. Her work powerfully illustrates how 'health problems interweave with complex factors such as relationship breakdown, job loss and welfare reform' (Garthwaite, 2016a, p 40). Garthwaite reports how anxiety is exacerbated by having to attend the food bank, adding to recipients' problems, and that interviewees reported acute embarrassment at the prospect of coming to the food bank (p 40). She concludes that it was common for food bank users to have experienced 'ill health, bereavement, relationship breakdown, substantial caring responsibilities or job loss', meaning that

> Deepening struggles with mental health inhibited other coping mechanisms or exacerbated wider crises, leading to a further worsening for some of already poor health. (p 42)

For Garthwaite, 'receipt of food aid is an extreme manifestation of poverty and inequality' (p 5), yet it could be argued that food banks have become somewhat normalised in the UK. The employment of poverty propaganda, sometimes in the form of outright lies about out-of-work benefit claimants and the causes of poverty in the current context, has meant that food banks have managed to slip into the public consciousness in ways that provoke responses that tend more towards puzzlement or indifference rather than outrage or disgust.

Conclusions

Poverty is inevitably associated with hardship and struggle. Research undertaken with those experiencing poverty shows that it is difficult to meet everyday needs, and debt is often inevitable as people struggle to meet not just everyday essential needs but additional necessary expenditure, such as for replacing everyday household items or in order to buy for birthdays and Christmas. The low level of 'welfare' benefits and low wages mean that more and more families are experiencing poverty, but their struggles remain largely hidden behind the sorts of rhetoric that we explored in Chapter Two. 'Welfare' reforms have brought significant hardship to those claiming 'welfare', putting people into a punishing system whereby 'welfare' payments are being withdrawn altogether for increasing numbers of people. The traumas associated with poverty, which include the increased risk of ill health and a greater propensity to early death, are allowed to remain hidden behind a rhetoric that depicts living on out-of-work 'benefits' as desirable, comfortable and easy when in reality it is anything but.

FOUR

Poverty, labour markets and 'poor work'

Introduction

> Over the last forty years, rising numbers of the workforce have been denied access to secure, decently paid work with reasonable prospects. A sizeable proportion of jobs available today are part-time, poorly paid, temporary and offer very limited opportunities for further progress. (Lansley and Mack, 2015, p 95)

> "Everybody needs to understand that you need to work for a living. You can't just expect everything for free, simple as that. It's important to work, without a doubt. Doesn't matter what it is. Cleaning **** out of the toilets, as long as I'm earning money for my family, I'd do it." (Kieran, aged 20, claiming JSA, Teesside interviewee in Shildrick et al, 2012b)

> "It was just the accepted thing. You went out to work ... My ambitions sort of faded because I was working in a factory. I didn't have much time for ambitions. I was working too hard." (Patrick, aged 49, Teesside interviewee in Shildrick et al, 2012b)

Paid employment holds a special place in poverty propaganda and it also has an important place in properly understanding the causes of poverty in the current social and economic context. Much poverty propaganda rests on the supposed distinction between those who are willing to work for their livelihoods and those who are purported to prefer to remain on out-of-work benefits. When George Osborne (Chancellor of the Exchequer 2010–16) asked, 'where is the fairness for the shift-worker leaving home in the dark hours of the early morning who looks up at the closed blinds of the next door neighbour sleeping off a life on benefits?' (Osborne, 2012), he was working to both create and perpetuate poverty propaganda, in a deliberate misrepresentation of reality. In British politics the repeated reference to 'hard-working families', juxtaposed to the people depicted as 'sleeping a life away on benefits' or choosing benefits as 'a lifestyle choice' (Duncan Smith, 2014), is used to deliberately evoke a depiction of 'normal' and 'ordinary' families as against the supposedly feckless and work-shy. The notion of ordinariness resonates strongly with the vast majority of people in Britain who prefer to identify themselves as something akin to 'ordinary' (Savage et al, 2001). The strong theme of unfairness is played to full effect by Osborne in marking out the supposedly recalcitrant, lazy deviants who are portrayed as benefiting from the 'welfare' system by dint of doing nothing. The fact that millions of people experience poverty, despite their dogged commitment to working hard in paid employment that fails to raise them out of poverty, is an increasingly important piece of the poverty jigsaw in contemporary Britain; but as an issue it remains securely hidden behind the simply and easily digested rhetoric of poverty propaganda. Changes in working-class employment opportunities are rarely properly dissected and this is the issue that the present chapter contends with. As already noted, an overriding conclusion from many years of researching these sorts of issues in deprived neighbourhoods with high rates of worklessness is that it is very difficult indeed to find people who have never had a job or who choose a lifetime on out-of-work benefits (Shildrick et al, 2012a; 2012b) even when one is determinedly searching for them in some of the most deprived locales in the UK.

Global capitalism, neoliberalism and the growth of low-paid and insecure work

Between governments and politicians of all stripes there is pretty much blanket agreement that paid employment is the best way to escape poverty (DWP, 2012a; 2012b; 2014; 2015; 2016; May, 2017). The arguments are repeated time and time again, yet it is a very telling fact that most households in poverty have at least one family member in paid work (JRF, 2016). The divisive characterisation of the 'hard working families' or the so-called 'strivers' positioned very firmly in direct contrast to the supposed 'shirkers' or 'skivers' simply does not reflect the cold reality. The punitive nature of the current 'welfare' system ensures that people do not remain within the system for any length of time if there is any prospect this can be avoided. As we saw in the last chapter it is more often a case of those in sometimes quite desperate need being turned away from the system and denied adequate (or in some cases any) support, than of people comfortably languishing at home on meagre out-of-work benefits.

We have already established that where people can possibly find work – even that of very poor quality and pay – they will choose paid work over 'welfare'. But for some people and families in Britain it is increasingly the case that the jobs they are able to access are unable to lift them out of poverty either far enough or for long enough to actually make a real difference to their lives (Goulden, 2010; Shildrick et al, 2010; 2012a; JRF, 2016). The labour market in Britain, broadly in line with those of many other developed countries, has changed dramatically since the mid-1970s (Giddens, 1999; Green et al, 2015). The labour force has grown and more women have entered paid employment, but the manufacturing sector, where working-class people traditionally found employment, has shrunk severely (Green, 2013; Beatty and Fothergill, 2016). This has happened at the same time as the deregulation of the labour market, which has been in train since the mid-1970s, a key outcome of which is the growth and structural embedding within employment of what is commonly described as 'poor work' (Byrne, 2005; Shildrick et al, 2012) – low-paid work, often in the service sector, that does not allow people to escape poverty or to have a decent standard of living.

Green and colleagues (2015) have undertaken research looking at changes in job quality in Britain in the 25 years since 1990. They point out that

> As well as decent pay, a 'good job' offers the scope for development and for taking initiative and some control over one's tasks, the prospect of a reasonable work load, safe and pleasant working conditions, good social support from colleagues and superiors, opportunities for participation in organizational decision making (whether direct or through the 'voice' of a union), and the flexibility to arrange working hours reasonably to balance one's work and non-work lives. 'Bad jobs' offer none or few of these. (Green et al, 2015, p 1)

The outcomes of globalisation processes at a European level have been described by Frazer and colleagues (2011, p 2), who argue that they have produced significant 'structural changes in the organisation of economic and social models', with 'deep changes in economic, employment and social spheres' across many developed countries. The growth of the knowledge-based economy and the commitment to the free market have also produced an increase in precarious employment, meting out this form of work to more people (Standing, 2014; 2016) and for extended periods of their working lives (Shildrick et al, 2012a). It is not just the nature of jobs that has changed: deregulation of the labour market has resulted in structural changes to the conditions of work. Both of these shifts have dramatic and lasting implications for working-class employment opportunities and possibilities. In countries like Britain free market capitalism has been supported by the deregulation of employment and an increase in segments of the labour market that do not have access to significant worker protections. This includes a growing number of workers on zero hours contracts (ONS, 2017), agency workers (Judge and Tomlinson, 2016) and those classed as self-employed (Tomlinson and Corlett, 2017). D'Arcy and Finch (2017) have shown that for many workers low-paid work is not acting as a stepping-stone to better jobs. Just as I found in my own research (Shildrick et al, 2012a), D'Arcy and Finch found that the first rung on the employment ladder remains just that: a first and only rung. Their study found that, of those in low-paid work in 2006, just one in six (17%) were what they call 'escapers' 10 years later in 2016. One in four (25%) remained stuck in low-paid jobs throughout the period, while a significant number (48%) were what they term 'cyclers' (D'Arcy and Finch, 2017, p 4).

The same cycling in and out of low-paid, short-term jobs and on and off benefits was the dominant experience amongst our interviewees (Shildrick et al, 2012a). It was a concern to test out this stepping-stone theory that drove our 'low pay, no pay' study (Shildrick et al, 2012a). The frequent refrain from politicians in respect of low-paid work is that it can provide a stepping-stone to something better, that prospective workers need to be prepared to accept poorer working conditions in order to achieve long-term gains in terms of their labour market position. Yet research very clearly shows that for some workers the low pay, no pay cycle will be the defining feature of their whole working lives (Shildrick et al, 2012a). Thompson points out that

> One aspect of low paid work that is particularly concerning is the link to employment insecurity. Those working for low wages tend also to be working in jobs characterised by temporary contracts and low hours and are more likely to experience individual barriers to employment security, such as work limiting health conditions and few qualifications. (Thompson, 2015, p 2)

As a consequence many workers find it well-nigh impossible to escape the cycle, just as D'Arcy and O'Connor (2017) show in their recent research. Part of the problem is that low-paid and insecure work can in itself be debilitating and damaging to people's health and well-being. Repeatedly having to engage in job search, just in order to access the first rung of the labour market ladder and then be knocked off, then to have to scrabble back on again as best one can, is time-consuming and far from easy. Some of the older interviewees in our research had been engaged in this low pay, no pay cycle for the majority of their working lives and many were acutely aware of the ways in which pay and labour market conditions had deteriorated over that time (Shildrick et al, 2012a).

Evidence is emerging that employment in 'poor work' is damaging not just for employees but for business and society more broadly. Green and colleagues point out that while the relationship between 'work, income inequality and social cohesion is complex' (Green et al, 2015, p 2) the evidence is very clear that poor working conditions are bad for individuals' physical and mental health and for society more broadly (Wilkinson and Pickett, 2010). Chandola and Zhang (2017) have demonstrated that previously unemployed adults who transition into poor-quality work experience higher markers of stress in comparison to those who remain unemployed, suggesting that poor job quality, in and of itself, may well have an adverse impact on well-being.

The low pay, no pay cycle is not simply a problem of recession or austerity (although these are very likely to have exacerbated the problem), as low-paid work and in-work poverty are now endemic in the British labour market. Gregg and Gardiner point out that

> Although initially connected to the downturn, some of the growth in these atypical or undesirable employment forms appears to have structural as well as cyclical elements. Therefore, we conclude that while the *breadth* of insecurity appears fairly stable over time – as best we can capture it with inevitably high-level data – the *depth* of precariousness faced by a significant minority has risen in this same period. (Gregg and Gardiner, 2015, p 6)

As Bivand and Melville (2017) show, the number of insecure workers rose from 2.4 million in 2011 to 3.1 million in 2016, so that by 2016 one in ten of those employed were in insecure employment. Furthermore, the authors also confirm that insecure employees are only half as likely to be supported by trade unions as are secure employees

– over the 2011–16 period only 14% of insecure employees were in workplaces covered by trade union representation, as compared to 30% among secure employees.

The low pay, no pay cycle is increasingly supported by the rise of the so called 'gig-economy', which is characterised by zero hours contracts whereby there is no formal agreement as to how many hours the employer will offer the employee or how many hours the employee will undertake to work. This is a particularly murky practice that allows extremely difficult working conditions to flourish. As Frances O'Grady, General Secretary of the Trades Union Congress (TUC), argues:

> For many workers the gig economy is a rigged economy, where bosses can get out of paying the minimum wage and providing basics like holidays and rest breaks. (O'Grady, 2016)

The Office for National Statistics (ONS) uses Labour Force Survey data to estimate the number of people on zero hours contracts and estimated in November 2016 that there were 1.7 million contracts that did not guarantee a minimum number of hours each week, representing 6% of all employment contracts (ONS, 2017). During October–November 2016, 905,000 people, or 2.8% of people in employment, were employed on this sort of contract (ONS, 2017). Thirty-two per cent of people said that they wanted to work more hours. While official estimates are likely to be an under-representation, these figures indicate that significant numbers of people are forced to cope with extreme insecurity in their work conditions. While this insecurity may be welcome for some people – such as older workers who want to supplement their retirement pension and are not reliant on a full-time income to survive, or students who may appreciate some flexibility in terms of the hours they work – for many workers the insecurity is 'a complete nightmare because you don't know what you are doing from one week to the next' (Rowlingson, 2015). Research also shows that a significant number of agency workers face major labour market disadvantages, including low pay and few workers' rights (Judge and Tomlinson, 2016). These workers tend to be clustered in the lower-skilled segments of the labour market and the majority would prefer to be in a full-time job (Judge and Tomlinson, 2016).

Engagement in low-paid employment is not evenly spread across the population. As we will see in the next chapter, the labour market is highly stratified according to social class, and those from low social-class backgrounds are much more likely to find themselves trapped in insecure and low-paid employment (Shildrick et al, 2012a) and unable to move away from poverty for any sustained period of time. Part of the problem is the compounding nature of poverty and its effects that work to limit opportunities, from birth, through education and onwards into the jobs market.

Things can be done differently. In 2016 New Zealand passed a Bill through Parliament to ban zero hours contracts (Ainge Roy, 2016). There is little sign that the UK is likely to follow suit any time soon, and more regularly we hear political figures insisting that zero hours contracts have benefits for employees, although there is very little evidence that those forced to rely on them would agree. Interestingly, in New Zealand the arguments that were put forward and that led to the ban emphasised the importance of 'fair and productive workplaces'. Despite many people's unhappiness with their zero hours contracts, a commitment to work over 'welfare' means that there is no shortage of people willing to take on this sort of work, but the evidence would suggest that for a significant number of such workers the contracts mean insecurity and exploitation rather than flexibility and choice.

As Jones (2011) describes it, more and more people are 'earning their poverty', and it is not just insecure work that is problematic but also low pay, and the two issues are often found to go hand in hand. Low pay is a complex issue, as not everyone in a low-paid job will live in a family experiencing poverty (for example, a middle-aged, middle-class person working part-time in a shop may receive a low wage but may also have other incomes coming into their household, and possibly also savings and/or inherited wealth). None the less, low pay is a particularly important issue in understanding poverty in the contemporary context.

Low pay and in-work poverty are relatively marginal in political and public debates on poverty. Corlett and Gardiner point out that 'even before the financial crisis hit too many employees in Britain were low paid by the standards of the day and relative to other countries' (Corlett and Gardiner, 2015, p 4). Growth in the numbers of people in low-paid jobs is one of the most significant factors to affect the British labour market since the mid-1990s (Yoon and Chung, 2016). The so-called National Living Wage (NLW), announced in 2015 by then Chancellor George Osborne and introduced in April 2016, was a purely deceptive measure (Veit-Wilson, 2015) designed to seduce the public into believing the rhetoric of a self-styled 'party of the workers' in the hope that the realities of low-paid, insecure employment would continue unabated and largely unnoticed. ONS estimates that in 2016 there were 362,000 jobs paying less than either the National

Minimum Wage or the NLW, and suggested that these constituted 1.3% of employee jobs in the UK.

A further problem is that since the onset of the recession in 2008 there has been increased competition for low-paid and insecure jobs. Unemployment and, importantly, under-employment are becoming a major problem (ONS, 2016). As unemployment increases, better-qualified people are forced down the employment ladder, placing further pressure on those already at the bottom. In the UK it is estimated that 10% of workers (around three million) are under-employed (ONS, 2016). Elementary occupations, including cleaning, bar work, sales and security, are the largest group of occupations where the under-employed are located (ONS, 2016). The group is further segmented by age, with just under 20% of 16- to 24-year-olds being under-employed in 2014, and by gender, with 11% of female workers being under-employed in 2014, as compared with 8.9% of male workers (ONS, 2016). Increasingly the labour market in Britain, as elsewhere, might best be described as 'a "buyers market" that operates in contrast to a "sellers market" which occurs when there is a shortage of labour' (Cote, 2014, p 84). Aguiar writes of these shifts in job quality that were in train even before the financial crisis hit:

> Many workers suffer lowered wages, the intensification of work, growing job insecurities, labour market precariousness and having to take on increased responsibilities without corresponding increases in compensation. (Aguiar, 2006, p 440)

In the past, employment legislation and collective bargaining (largely by the working classes) meant that more jobs became more secure and carried workers' rights such as pensions and sick pay. Since the 1980s and the inception of a neoliberal policy environment, these working-class gains have been undermined in many segments of the labour market. The deliberate undermining of the unions and the weakening both of workers' rights and of collective bargaining power mean that working conditions have deteriorated and insecurity is now an integral feature of many layers of the labour market, spreading the risks of poverty more widely. Indeed many of the jobs that constitute 'poor work', in sectors such as catering and care work, disallow union representation. In addition to stress and anxiety, the insecurity of such work often presents people with difficulties in managing their day-to-day finances, with a knock-on effect on managing day-to-day life (Hay, 2015; Shildrick et al, 2012a).

Ordinary workers have been immiserated (Herod and Aguiar, 2006, p 428) by the outsourcing of many low-paid jobs such as cleaning, which means greater competition for jobs and greater intensification of work. Risks have been moved away from capital and the state and on to the shoulders of individual workers, and insecurity in many different forms has increased significantly (Orton, 2014). Working-class job opportunities have been completely reshaped, with widespread implications for the working class in Britain, who now find themselves increasingly at risk of in-work poverty.

Hard work, poverty and insecurity: experiencing poor work

One of the overriding findings of the research that I have undertaken is the commitment to work that characterises interviewees' life stories (Shildrick et al, 2012a). Our interviewees described working in a range of jobs, often in the service sector, including shop work, care work and catering as well as manufacturing and production-line work. While our interviewees spoke positively about being in work – and it was a desire to be in work rather than out of work and reliant on out-of-work benefits that drove their long-term commitment to it – they also undertook work that was hard and often unrewarding in many different ways, not just financially (Shildrick et al, 2012a). Research for the JRF has also looked at the feelings and experiences of low-paid workers in the care, hospitality and retail industries (Hay, 2015). It reported that workers 'tended to be deeply conscious of their place at the bottom of (workplace) hierarchies' (Hay, 2015, p 3). The research also found that workers lacked awareness of rights and opportunities and had little awareness of the existence of workplace unions that might have assisted in improving their working lives (p 3). Workers reported problems with pay, relationships with line managers and also the 'stress and physicality of jobs' (Hay, 2015, p 4). Care work in particular was consistently described as 'exhausting and very physically demanding' (p 29). Many of the jobs that are low paid and insecure are ones that are physically hard and sometimes dirty or dangerous. Crucially, they provide essential labour that allows our society to function properly and successfully. As a report by the Equality and Human Rights Commission (EHRC) has noted:

> The cleaning sector contributes over 8 billion pounds to the British economy every year. It provides a vital service to us all ensuring our workplaces, hospitals, schools, transport

and public spaces are clean and pleasant to use. (EHRC, 2014, p 6)

Referring to a 'largely invisible workforce', in which even the workers describe themselves and their work as 'invisible' and 'the lowest of the low' (EHRC, 2014, p 8), the report states that the sector is rife with discrimination and poor employment practices. It goes on to state that while there are some examples of very good practice, 'many workers, however, do not have their employment rights upheld. They may be bullied or discriminated against by supervisors, experience problems obtaining their pay, have excessive workloads and are not treated with dignity and respect' (EHRC, 2014, p 6). In fact, problems receiving the correct pay for the hours worked are perpetual (EHRC, 2014, p 6). Similar accounts have been found in other research with low-paid workers (Shildrick et al, 2012). The EHRC's research into the cleaning sector found that pay in general terms was low and getting lower, with 'overtime and weekend rates being abolished' (EHRC, 2014, p 30), and concluded that 'systemic underpayment' exists in the sector (p 36). One of the respondents stated:

> "I am having difficulty getting my wages. This is a problem which has been on-going throughout the term of my employment lasting 9 months. Given that I live in poverty at the best of times delayed payments can have a significant impact resulting in having to walk to the university which is quite some distance away, as well as go without food for the day." (EHRC, 2014, p 37)

In our research it was common to hear interviewees report a raft of injustices and seemingly unfair treatment of low-paid workers. Our interviewees tended to report injustices, and at times apparently illegal behaviours, with little complaint and in weary tones of acceptance. Many relayed these experiences as just "the way it is" and, given their desire to be in work rather than out of it, they tended to accept whatever they were faced with and, of course, they mostly felt they had little choice. Interviewees told us of numerous instances of being asked to undertake work at short notice and of not being paid properly for hours undertaken and when the wages were usually desperately needed. Occasionally they expressed anger and frustration at their treatment, but most knew that they had little opportunity for redress. Even more rarely interviewees did manage to challenge workplace injustice. One interviewee described to us how he had led a revolt of workers at a turkey factory in Teesside (now closed, but over many years a key employer of many of our interviewees) after many weeks of being short-changed in their pay packets in the run-up to Christmas. He recounted the incident with some pleasure and triumph, and it was indeed a rather lighter episode in his life story of hard work and low pay in many different jobs and over many, many years (Shildrick et al, 2010; 2012a).

Some of our interviewees also reported that they had been injured in the course of their work. Injuries were often ignored, downplayed or overlooked by employers (Shildrick et al, 2010). It is important to note that this sort of work is often fraught with risks that are rarely balanced with employee protections or adequate attention to health and safety. Herod and Aguiar (2006) have argued that cleaning is 'one of the most injury-prone occupations in the contemporary labour market' (p 426). They also point out that

> Despite such low pay and harsh conditions, though, cleaners are situated at an important nexus of the global economy, for they are essential to ensuring the spaces of production, consumption and social reproduction which define the social architecture of the contemporary global economy remain sanitary and functional. Indeed without their labor, the offices, factories, hospitals, shopping malls, sporting arenas and other spaces of the modern global economy would soon become buried under a surfeit of paper, metal shavings, medical waste, plastic packaging, and other assorted detritus of economic activity. (Herod and Aguiar, 2006, p 427)

The propensity of some employers to treat their workers badly was exemplified in the UK in 2016 by the case of Mike Ashley, the owner of Sports Direct, a cheap sports clothing company. After allegations of astonishingly bad practices at one of his factories were widely reported in the press, Mike Ashley finally agreed to appear before a parliamentary select committee to answer the allegations. The request for him to appear was issued in March 2016, but he finally agreed to speak to the committee only in July 2016. Iain Wright MP, Chair of the Business, Innovation and Skills Committee, said after the hearing in July 2016:

> Whistleblowers, parts of the media and a trade union shone a light on work practices at Sports Direct and what they revealed was extremely disturbing. The evidence we heard

points to a business whose working practices are closer to that of a Victorian workhouse than that of a modern, reputable High Street retailer. For this to occur in the UK in 2016 is a serious indictment of the management at Sports Direct and Mike Ashley, as the face of Sports Direct, must be held accountable for these failings. It seems incredible that Mike Ashley, who visits the Shirebrook warehouse at least once a week, was unaware of these appalling practices. This suggests Mr Ashley was turning a blind eye to conditions at Sports Direct in the interests of maximizing profits or that there are serious corporate governance failings which left him out of the loop in spite of all the evidence. Mike Ashley had to be brought kicking and screaming to answer the Committee's questions about working practices at Sports Direct. (Wright, 2016)

The committee heard evidence about workers denied breaks and penalised for being ill, and there were even allegations that permanent contracts had been offered in return for sexual favours. The widespread attention given to this particular case might lead some to conclude it was an isolated case, but this is far from being so. Research into the meat-processing industry demonstrates how that industry 'brings millions of pounds to the British economy' (EHRC, 2010, p 1), yet it relies heavily on agency workers and there is 'widespread evidence of poor treatment of agency workers, particularly migrant and pregnant workers' (EHRC, 2010, p 1). The research concluded that many 'endure even physical and verbal abuse without complaint' (EHRC, 2010, p 1). The widespread mistreatment of workers included prevention from using the toilets, 'including pregnant women, women with heavy periods and people with bladder problems'. Many workers pointed to the 'lasting humiliation of workers urinating and bleeding on themselves while working at the production line' (EHRC, 2010, p 11). As in many other studies, the research also reported the effects of insecurity of employment:

"Even now, 10 months on, I wouldn't be surprised to get a 'phone call. The insecurity, literally the financial insecurity, is terrible. You can't plan nothing when you have got no money; you can't do nothing because you don't know how long it's got to last you." (EHRC, 2010, p 9)

The extent of mistreatment of workers of the sort noted above is difficult to gauge because the problem is largely hidden. That there is no shortage of people willing to undertake such work is indicative of the resilience of the work ethic that has come through so strongly and persistently in all of my own research (Shildrick, 2012a; MacDonald et al, 2013). Poor working opportunities and conditions, in the form of zero hours contracts, split shifts, low pay, no right to paid holidays and the lack of other elements of working life that serve to make employment better for workers, are an increasingly significant part of the British labour market. The existence of these working practices, their extent and their role in causing poverty for significant numbers of workers and their families must be brought into clearer sight. In the Sports Direct case the unions played a crucial role in bringing the case into the open, yet the unions had also seen a virtual collapse of their relationship with the management of Sports Direct. The reason for this collapse (as has been the case with unions more broadly) was the massive shift away from permanently employed staff and towards agency workers at Sports Direct since 2008 (Goodley, 2016). The deregulation of the labour market has facilitated practices that favour 'owners' over 'workers'. These trends towards low-paid, insecure employment have regional as well as classed dimensions and the following section looks at the regional aspects more closely.

Working-class employment opportunities: the importance of place

A key change in the labour market over the last four decades has been the major restructuring of the working-class labour market that began in the era of the Thatcher government, resulting in 'profound restructuring and 'de-industrialisation' (Green et al, 2015, p 3). This restructuring has had an uneven geographical impact, with localities that were heavily reliant on particular heavy industries, for example the steel works and the coal mines, being particularly badly affected. This has important implications for understanding the geography of poverty and the ways in which some groups and communities are more at risk than others. Beatty and Fothergill have charted this change in the economy and the risks for particular places since the late 1970s, and they conclude that

> In the UK, the defining feature of the economy over the last thirty or forty years has been the big shift away from industry as an employer and generator of wealth. That this

'deindustrialisation' has happened is widely understood. It is part of the backdrop to modern life. Yet the massive consequences for the contemporary economy and for present-day policy-making are generally overlooked. This is unfortunate because major economic changes, such as deindustrialisation, have impacts that spill over from decade to decade. (Beatty and Fothergill, 2016, p 3)

The changing structure of the labour market has global roots, and manufacturing has been in decline for a long time in many countries. The manufacturing base of the UK economy shrank from 26.1% of total jobs in 1979 to just 8.9% in 2011 and the number remains at around 8% at the time of writing (ONS, 2017). The sector was estimated to be worth £8.9 million in the mid-1960s and in 2016 was worth £2.9 million (Beatty and Fothergill, 2016). The expansion of white-collar jobs and the service sector that ran alongside the decline of heavy industry has been lauded as evidence of upward social mobility (for those who once did manual manufacturing work) and is often offered as evidence of a decline in class inequality. We probe these issues further in the following chapter but, as Beatty and Fothergill show, the consequence of the destruction of the industrial base in particular places and particular areas is large numbers of people being shifted towards 'welfare', through either unemployment or ill health (Beatty and Fothergill, 2016). Furthermore, it has rendered others reliant on short-term, low-paid jobs that trap them in the low pay, no pay cycle (Shildrick et al, 2012a). This uneven geographical impact is generally missing from policy and political debates, but it is absolutely crucial if we are to understand the uneven geography of poverty and inequality in contemporary Britain.

It is important not to paint an overly romantic picture of a past where heavy industry always provided secure work, nor to deny the fact that such work was often downright dirty, dangerous and very difficult. As already noted, much of my own research has been conducted on Teesside. As we see below, it is a place that provides fascinating insight into the changing economic and social fortunes of a place and its people. Over a century ago Lady Bell, a writer and playwright, noted in her study of the steel industry on Teesside:

Many workers were absolutely poor. More were so near the poverty line that they were constantly passing over it. Life for a third of these workers is an unending struggle

from day to day to keep abreast of the most ordinary needs.
(Bell, 1907)

Over 100 years later I found myself writing something not wholly dissimilar when preparing a report for JRF from our project on recurrent poverty:

> The predominant experience was of moving in and out of low paying jobs but never moving far from poverty ...//... Wider aspects of disadvantage (e.g. ill health) led interviewees to lose and leave jobs ...//... day-to-day life was a juggling act and interviewees faced significant financial hardship. (Shildrick et al, 2010)

What is perhaps most interesting about the two extracts is that they represent two periods of time between which there was a rise in general standards of living and an increase in workers' rights and protections, yet, despite the gains in the interim we can see that paid work continues to be site of deep struggle for those on the margins of the labour market.

The geography of the distribution of precarious and poor work is important. In London, for example, where the economy is reliant on migrant labour to 'clean its offices, care for its sick, make beds and serve at its restaurants and bars', the profile of low-paid, insecure workers looks very different from that in older industrial localities (Wills, 2010, p 29). London's reliance on foreign-born workers to do the worst, but vitally important, jobs in the British labour market will face added challenges as the UK moves to leave the EU. But it is the older, industrial regions that have fared especially badly in respect of the decline of heavy industry, as the economies of some places are now dominated by low-paid and insecure jobs, with a paucity of higher-skilled and professional jobs. Decent employment opportunities (of the sort described above by Green and colleagues) in many of these regions have been incrementally reduced. While the causes of poverty have become almost wholly individualised in popular and political narratives, almost wholly dominated by poverty propaganda, the story of what has happened – and, most importantly, of what has actively been done – to particular places in terms of employment opportunities often goes unmentioned. This geographical unevenness of opportunity is neatly summed up by Innes when he suggests that

> Rising employment is encouraging and provides the best route to economic security for low-income families. But

we know a burgeoning jobs market alone will not lift the poorest people and places out of poverty. Despite record employment levels nationally, in the Northern Powerhouse regions the proportion of working age adults in work remains below the UK average, and the lion's share of jobs growth is clustered around a booming London and the south. In contrast to the southeast, the employment rate in Yorkshire and the Humber actually fell back on last year, showing some of the weaknesses the northern regions still face. (Innes, 2016)

The history of employment has class and cultural dimensions as well as economic ones. Decisions were taken to close particular industries that were neither inevitable nor, some would argue, economically sensible in the longer term. The closure of the coal mines during the 1980s after a series of high-profile strikes was a crucial and critical moment in the history of working-class life in Britain, as well as in working-class politics. The high visibility of what took place during the strikes, particularly the brutality of the clashes between the police and the striking miners, and the subsequent closure of the pits not only heralded a seismic shift in the manufacturing base that had supported the working class (albeit with work that was hard, dirty and often dangerous) but paved the way for the reshaping of the working class itself. Buckley describes the miners' strikes as 'one of the most embittered disputes in the history of British industrial relations, which still divides families, former colleagues and entire communities' (Buckley, 2015, p 420). The impact of the loss of the mines on the people and their communities was both immediate and long lasting.

The long-standing impacts of these changes to the economic infrastructure in particular places cannot be over-estimated and it is such changes that have been laid bare in much of my own research The gradual winding-down of the steel industry in Redcar on Teesside represents only the latest development in over four decades of industrial decline that has blighted the region. As with the coalmines, the decision to finally close the steelworks in 2015 was political rather than simply economic, despite the rhetoric to the contrary: there were real possibilities for revitalisation and innovation. Allwood has noted how the UK could lead innovation in the steel industry 'ahead of any other large player' (Allwood, 2016) by adopting new technology and investing in recycled steel. The European Commission has also argued that investment could have saved Redcar, and the steel industry more broadly. It points out that 'the current challenges for the steel industry are serious, but they can be overcome if all players work together in a spirit of true co-operation' (European Commission, 2016). The refusal to invest in the steel industry, with its overt and explicitly working-class heritage, plain for all to see, can be contrasted with the approach taken to the banking industry (Shildrick, 2015). The class and cultural differences between government ministers and steel workers have both explicit and implicit signifiers of inequality and class (Shildrick, 2015).

> The contrast between that image (of the steel works and its working class heritage) and some of the sharply dressed government Ministers who eventually found their way to Redcar (and who were usually interviewed outside of the works) was at times almost palpable. Ministers often looked – and quite likely felt – out of place. People of the social class background that make up much of this current government simply do not belong in places like Redcar. It's an uncomfortable truth, but it's a truth all the same. (Shildrick, 2015)

It is difficult not to conclude that 'It may well just be an unfortunate coincidence that the bankers share more class heritage with those in the government than the steel workers, but on the other hand it might not' (Shildrick, 2015). The Conservative Party's 2017 election manifesto begins to talk about plans for a long overdue industrial policy, but it is also very explicit that this will not be 'about propping up failing industries' (Conservative and Unionist Party, 2017). Not only have traditional working-class industrial jobs been destroyed – some would argue, unnecessarily – but the jobs (and thus the people who once did those jobs) are also cleverly portrayed as failing, lacking or lagging behind and hankering for outdated ways of working. This stereotyping of jobs, as well as of the people associated with them, feeds into the wider narratives of failure that now surround the working classes and what they are purported to have become. The working class and the jobs that had once supported their lives and communities were assigned to become relics of the past, with lasting implications for the people and the places affected by these far-reaching changes to working-class job opportunities.

These issues of long-term industrial decline are exemplified in Middlesbrough, the town where I did much of my own research. Middlesbrough provides an interesting example of a once-thriving industrial, largely working-class conurbation that has declined as the industries that supported it have closed or been vastly scaled back. It is perhaps an archetypical example of a town that has risen and fallen according to shifts in the economy and policy decisions made by various governments. The change from a vibrant and expanding industrial manufacturing base in the steel and other heavy industries, to a far less vibrant and often struggling service economy has played out to full effect in Teesside, as in other similar towns up and down the UK. Moreover, the effects of these changes are writ large on the altered life opportunities of the people who continue to live there (Webster et al, 2004; MacDonald and Marsh, 2005; Shildrick and MacDonald, 2007; Shildrick and MacDonald, 2008; Shildrick et al, 2012a; 2012b). These changes have significant implications for poverty and for working-class employment security. Guy Standing, is his book *The Precariat Charter*, neatly captures the impressive scale and reach of Middlesbrough's past:

> In 2013 I was invited to present *The Precariat* in Middlesbrough, a birthplace of the Industrial Revolution in the 19th century, which in a few years went from being a nondescript hamlet to a hub of the economy of the British Empire (Heggie, 2013). It was the site of the first ironworks, later branching into steel and chemicals. Statues of the figures who built the industries stand in the town centre; plaques marking some personality or place remind the visitor of a proud past. Australia's Sydney Harbour Bridge and San Francisco's Golden Gate Bridge were built in or near Middlesbrough, as was much of the Indian Railway system. On a gate is emblazoned: 'Born of iron, made of steel'. (Standing, 2014, p 319)

Contrasting this industrial and prosperous past with the marked and obvious evidence of decline that is symbolised in the old town hall – 'derelict on a hill, surrounded by wasteland and weeds' (Standing, 2014, p 319) – Standing makes an important moral and economic point about the contribution made by Middlesbrough's workers (many of whom migrated there to work) to the wealth and prosperity of our country today. In making the argument for a basic income for all, he notes that

> Still 140,000 people continue to live in the town. They suffer the cruelty of history. The wealth today of those living in the South of England and in other affluent parts of the country was generated in part by the people of Middlesbrough. Why should people living in these well-endowed places have lives so much more comfortable and

secure than the descendants of those who built the country's wealth and power? (Standing, 2014, pp 319–20)

In making this significant point Standing shows the importance of taking a historical perspective if we truly want to understand the present. While some jobs have been created in Teesside and places like it, they are of the sort that were described earlier in this chapter, and hence decent employment opportunities in these places are limited in number. 'Lousy jobs' and those in the 'gig economy' are pretty much in relative abundance. In our Teesside youth transitions studies, our interviewees had witnessed at first hand the generational effects of the changing employment opportunities and landscape, and we concluded that while young people retained highly conventional attitudes and aspirations for the future, the 'economic scaffolding' around them had collapsed (Webster et al, 2004, p 36). Our interviewees were not work-shy: they wanted to and did work. They embraced whatever work they could get, but while most did get jobs, these were mostly short term and low paid, with implications for their ability to support and progress decent working-class lives, both in and out of work (Webster et al, 2004; MacDonald and Marsh, 2005; Shildrick et al, 2012). Similarly Bright's research with young people living in former pit villages has shown how they continue to bear the impacts of the pit closures in their communities. Using the notion of 'social haunting', Bright shows how young people, in particular, are affected by this 'terminal period of the UK deep coalmining industry' (Bright, 2016, p 142).

> The central argument of all of my work since 2006 has basically been that aspects of the 1984–1985 miners' strike and its aftermath of pit closures are not just matters of historical interest, but are, rather, a continuing – if more often than not unspoken – *affective context* for the lived experiences for thousands of young people within Britain's former coalfields. (Bright, 2016, p 143)

Bright's work powerfully illustrates the difficulties faced by young people who, historically, would have found work of one sort or another in the pits and whose families had traditionally worked there too. They find themselves at odds with an education system that does not serve them well. All too often they are excluded from school and face numerous other problems and disadvantages, many of which can be traced back to the history of work in their communities (Bright, 2016). The structurally embedded lack of opportunities is key to understanding how lives play out over time. Young people living in areas that are dominated by poor work, who suffer the injuries of poverty and related disadvantages, face a mountain of obstacles to get better jobs, the main one being the lack of decent jobs available to them. We know that the current younger generation as a whole faces diminishing opportunities in comparison with their parents' generation and may well be the first to live through a decline rather than an improvement in their life conditions, leading some to argue that they are a 'jilted generation' (Howker and Malik, 2010). But these generational inequalities have intra-generational as well as inter-generational aspects as social class differences become more important for young people in places like Teesside.

Since the vote to leave the EU, it has been argued that in some of the older industrial areas it was a sense of being locked out of the benefits of market capitalism that prompted the vote to leave (Goodwin and Heath, 2016). While the vote to leave the EU was clearly very complex and the reasons behind what exactly drove the vote in either direction may never be fully revealed, it is very clear that people who have lived through industrial decline are neither ignorant nor indifferent as to the changes that have been wrought on their employment opportunities and their lives and life chances more broadly. Respondents in our research were often acutely aware and often painfully discerning about the industrial decline that had taken place over their lifetimes. Patrick, a Teesside interviewee in our 2012 study, told us "When I first left (school) it was good, in 1978 but I believe when Margaret Thatcher got in it changed overnight" (Patrick, aged 49, Teesside, in Shildrick et al, 2012b). Many of our older interviewees were clear that the Thatcher government was a period when their lives changed for the worse. Michelle, one of our Glasgow interviewees in the same study put it: "The Margaret Thatcher years I call it, that woman done something to the world". Some of our interviewees pointed to the apparent unfairness between the treatment of the bankers and that of the steel industry on Teesside:

> "The bankers had to be bailed out but the steel workers wanted too much money, but it was a lot less than what the bankers wanted and they wouldn't give 'em it. They had to shut the works down. Then the shops started closing, clubs started closing. It's like a vicious circle." (Ryan, 54, Teesside interviewee, in Shildrick et al, 2012b)

Other research has highlighted the diminution of employment opportunities and people's acute awareness of these processes:

> "I had a well-paid job. Try finding a job in this area that pays that kind of money (now). They just don't exist. There is the odd job (that's) good, well paid but there's literally thousands of applications for every job. The prospects up here – there's just nothing ...//... I'm speaking to the lads (who are) applying for dozens of jobs every week and getting nothing. They are good lads and wanting to work; there's just nothing for them." (Respondent cited in O'Hara, 2015a, pp 141–2)

This is not the place to interrogate how far these sorts of sentiments drove the vote to leave the EU, but what is perhaps clear from the evidence presented in this book so far is that life is not easy for those on low incomes, and few of those experiencing poverty and its related disadvantages and a lack of decent work opportunities are oblivious either to their existence or their unfairness. Those who live, work and make their lives in places like Teesside are not just aware of the changes that have been delivered on their doorsteps by successive governments over many decades; they live with the consequences through every day of their own and their families' lives.

Conclusions

Professor David Byrne (2005) provides a useful account of 'social exclusion' when he points to a group of workers engaged in 'poor work' as 'absolutely intrinsic' to post-industrial capitalism (Byrne, 2005, p 56). Rather than being a redundant, completely excluded group, many workers in the UK are moving repeatedly between low-paid jobs and 'welfare', largely as a consequence of the lack of better jobs (Byrne, 2005, p 56). In Byrne's work this group is described as a 'stagnant reserve army of labour' who are 'absolutely crucial' to the contemporary economy (p 56). As Beatty and Fothergill argue, the Treasury 'has misdiagnosed high welfare spending as the result of inadequate work incentives and has too often blamed individuals for their own predicament, whereas in fact a large part of the bill is rooted in job destruction extending back decades (Beatty and Fothergill, 2016, p 2). Since the mid-1970s Britain has pursued a form of free market capitalism that has resulted in significant wealth creation for the country and increases in living standards for many. But these gains have not been equally felt. While many have seen increases in their personal and family standards of living in general terms, those at the top of the income scale have seen their incomes increase at an astonishing rate (Dorling, 2016). For those who have been locked out or only occasionally allowed a glimpse of these benefits, working conditions have been gradually getting worse. Poor pay and insecurity have been spreading to more and more sectors of the labour market, with those on the lower echelons facing increasingly problematic conditions of employment that do not allow them to escape from poverty. The frequent refrain that work provides the best route out of poverty is beginning to sound decidedly hollow.

FIVE

Poverty, social class and social immobility

Introduction

> Class distinctions do not die; they merely learn new ways
> of expressing themselves. Each decade we shiftily declare
> we have buried class; each decade the coffin stays empty.
> (Richard Hoggart, 1989)

> The greatest injustice in Britain today is that your life is
> still largely determined not by your efforts and talents but
> by where you come from, who your parents are and what
> schools you attend. (Conservative and Unionist Party, 2017)

> "I wanted to be a forensic scientist when I left school
> (laughs) ...//... I ended up doing a childcare course. I
> got an apprenticeship in a private nursery when I first left
> school. Just an apprenticeship in a private nursery but I only
> did that for a bit, then I left to take full time care of my
> sister." (Trudy, aged 25, Teesside interviewee in Shildrick
> et al, 2012b)

The book so far has detailed examples of poverty propaganda and
talked about contemporary experiences of poverty, yet nothing has
explicitly been said about social class. Yet it is questions about social
class that lie at the heart of much of the discussion in this book. Peter
Townsend, one of the foremost researchers on poverty in the last
century, was interested in the ways in which social class and status
differences in society were organised in order to benefit some in
society at the expense of disadvantaging others (Townsend, 1975).
Social class can be measured in any number of different ways, but at
its heart is a question of economics. There is little question that since
the 1970s social class has become a complex, confused and contested
concept, with much debate over its meaning as well as its continued
relevance. In both political and popular arenas the concept has become

largely redundant amid social changes that have, on the surface at least, appeared to make the concept of class less vital. We will see below that this idea has been supported by a neoliberal agenda that prioritises the promotion of free choice along with the individualisation of life chances, experiences responsibilities (Beck, 2002).

Access to life opportunities is to a large degree still determined by social class background, but this unevenness of opportunity – and who benefits from this unevenness – is deliberately overshadowed by a focus on the opportunities themselves. Life biographies and life chances are largely presented – and thus, all too frequently understood – as being self-determined. The supposedly self-scripted lifestyle dominates in neoliberal capitalist societies and has become the largely accepted norm. Essentially, labour market changes (particularly deindustrialisation and the decline of traditional working-class employment) and general advances in living standards that until relatively recently were afforded to large segments of the population (Hood and Waters, 2017) combined with the increasing importance of consumption as a marker of social inclusion (Miles, 2009), have worked to produce changes in how people think and feel about social class, as well as shifts in how social class is configured and experienced (Savage et al, 2013; Savage, 2015). Class is essentially no less present but is less easy to define and sometimes less easy to see. The increasing propensity towards the stigmatisation and demonisation of the working class, particularly through poverty propaganda, leads to a situation whereby even those experiencing deep poverty prefer to disassociate and distance themselves from the condition (Shildrick and MacDonald, 2013). Far better to lean towards association with the messy middle than to align oneself with the undeserving. When political figures like Theresa May appeal to the 'mainstream' they are in effect astutely targeting a huge segment of the population, from those on middling incomes who have seen their living standards decline since 2008 (Hood and Joyce, 2017) to those on very low incomes who also, in their efforts to distance themselves from poverty and its associated disadvantages, tend to perceive themselves as 'just ordinary' or 'just managing' (Shildrick and MacDonald, 2013).

Individualisation, social class and the messy middle

There are a myriad of ways in which social class might be defined and it is not the intention of this chapter to rehearse well-worn debates (see Roberts, 2001; Bradley, 1996, 2013, 2014; Crompton, 1998; Skeggs, 2005; Savage et al, 2013; Savage, 2015). Erik Olin Wright argues that 'the principal way that most people understand the concept of class is in terms of individual attributes and life conditions' (Wright, E.O., 2015, p 3). Class is not just about economics and the material conditions of life but also has cultural and, increasingly, psychosocial dimensions (Walker and Chase, 2013; Mills, 2014). In this chapter it is the material conditions that dominate as we look at some of the ways in which social class is important for how we understand poverty and how it works to shape the distribution of life chances, shaping not just class distinctions, but also inequalities in the distribution of opportunity. Quite simply, social class works by affording class advantages or disadvantages depending on where in the class structure a person is located. For those experiencing poverty it is the disadvantages inherent in social class that are crucial in understanding poverty and its effects. Essentially, if poverty is to be properly understood it has to be understood as largely a classed experience. During the 1980s a series of arguments emerged that challenged the contemporary relevance of social class and that might be broadly clustered around the 'death of social class' thesis (Pakulski and Waters, 1997). In particular, the growing importance of the consumer society (Miles, 2009) led some to argue that traditional dimensions of inequality, such as social class, had receded in importance because widespread access to consumption allowed greater potential for the exercise of individual choice.

Debates continue over how far social class is important for life chances but it would be churlish, to say the least, to assert that class no longer matters. Indeed in a context of austerity and tightened economic circumstances that are set to become tighter following the UK's decision to leave the EU (Belfield et al, 2016) the struggle over resources will inevitably become even more competitive. It has been argued that inherited wealth (and other privileges associated with more affluent class positions) are set to become ever more, rather than less important (Hood and Joyce, 2017). One thing that is very clear, however, is that social class in the contemporary context is more messy and complex than it might have been in previous times. Savage and colleagues undertook the Great British Class Survey in 2013 in collaboration with the BBC (see Savage et al, 2013; 2015). There is not space to go into their findings in detail here (see Bradley, 2014; Dorling, 2014; Mills, 2014; Rollock, 2014; Standing, 2014) but one thing that is very clear from their research is that class today is lived and felt very differently to how it might have been in the past. For Savage and colleagues, classes are 'being fundamentally remade' (Savage, 2015, p 4) with stark disparities between the top ('the wealthy elite') and the bottom (what they define as the 'precariat') and 'much more complex and fuzzy' (Savage, 2015, p 4) middle layers. It is this class complexity, and particularly the growth of what I describe as a messy middle, that is so conducive to the proliferation and success of poverty propaganda. Back in the 1970s the 'spectre of embourgeoisement haunted the sociology of class' (Atkinson, 2010, p 1). As Roberts notes, the embourgeoisement thesis rests on an argument that as incomes rise members of the working class are able to buy and do things that formerly 'signalled middle class status' (Roberts, 2001, p 12). The thesis emerged largely as a consequence of changes in the employment structure outlined in the previous chapter (particularly the decline of traditional manual jobs), along with the spread of increasing consumption and general rising living standards.

The messy middle is aptly supported by the increasing pervasiveness of what might usefully be described as a 'middle class norm'. As Devine et al (2005, p 97) point out, 'In the 1970s it was largely agreed that the working class was characterised by distinctive values and practices which stood outside, and in opposition to, those of the middle and upper classes.' More recently, traditionally middle-class values have become the largely accepted norm (Gillies, 2005), and the working-class are increasingly required to 'masquerade as middle class' (Walkerdine et al, 2001, p 22). We see this shift in expectations in terms of the demands of longer periods in education and the ever-increasing demands for formal educational qualifications, even for low-paid and insecure jobs. We also see it in the emergence of consumption as a major marker of inequality amid the widespread pressure to consume that continues apace. The new cleavages around housing are also further evidence of this drift towards a supposed middle-class norm. Margaret Thatcher played a significant role in fostering the belief that homeownership was desirable and achievable, even for those on lower incomes. In selling off much of the council housing stock to tenants at remarkably low prices, she added significant weight to this emerging middle-class norm in terms of expectations, attitudes and values towards the home as a marker of success. In the current context, housing has become a critical site of class struggle (Watt, 2017). Young people increasingly require parental or family resources to buy their own homes, or more often remain locked out of the housing market all together (Hood and Joyce, 2017). Yet the power of the connotations of respectability that are still very much attached to homeownership remains as strong as ever. Societal expectations continue to dictate that homeownership is a marker of respectability, achievement and appropriate aspiration, and evidence shows that the vast majority of people (86%) would prefer to own their own home, and many cite affordability as the main barrier to achieving this (British Social Attitudes, 2017, p 28). The unevenness of access to decent housing remains largely hidden. The housing options open to working-class people have diminished and those on out-of-work benefits are being particularly hard hit, as we saw in Chapter Two (Watt, 2017).

These shifts have had huge ramifications for the working classes in Britain. As the employment base has shifted and given way to more messy class configurations, the working class has become harder to identify and, thus, the idea that the working class is somehow lagging, economically and culturally, becomes much easier to sustain. The working class has been successfully labelled as impoverished not just by their economic situations: 'theirs is also a cultural impoverishment, a poverty of identity based on out-dated ways of thinking and being' (Haylett, 2001, p 352). Haylett points out that

> The identification of the white working class poor as a barrier to the two-part process of 'multicultural modernisation' is pivotal to the contemporary process of national/welfare reform. It works to discriminate between non-problematic 'selves' and problematic 'others' who become ciphers (or a dumping ground) for the heavy contradictions of a multicultural 'welfare' society articulated within a neoliberal and middle-class imaginary. (Haylett, 2001, p 357)

These narratives of class stereotyping and prejudice are weighty, and thus the problem of the working class becomes one not of a lack of decent paid employment opportunities but one whereby the working class refuse to embrace new opportunities. The contemporary working class are neither aspirational enough nor motivated enough to 'get on' and thus remain stuck in a problematic, recalcitrant underbelly of society through, choice, idleness or a combination of the two. These new narratives are a long way from the traditional ways in which the working class were perceived. As Evans and Tilley point out:

> The mid-20th century saw the rise of the working class. Whether you were an angry young man of the 1950s literary scene, or a working class hero of '60s pop culture, it was good to be working class. People were proud of their working class status and working class background. (Evans and Tilley, 2015, p 1)

We have moved to a situation where the 'politics and social norms of 21st century Britain are about working-class marginalisation rather than working-class pride' (Evans and Tilley, 2015, p 298). Part of the explanation for this lies in the simple statistics. The vast majority of people used to fall broadly into the group that could be defined as working class. Todd points out that in 1910 the 'vast majority' (Todd, 2014, p 1) of people could be defined as (or identified with) being working class, and dubs the years 1910 to 2010 as the 'working class century' (p 1). She charts the rise of the 'economic and political clout of the working class' (p 2). There can be little doubt that the working class were important to the economy, could be called on in a crisis and could generally be relied upon to undertake hard and often unpleasant and (sometimes) downright dangerous work. The shift to service sector employment – combined with the other changes described above – has really worked to muddy and muddle class boundaries. Roberts rightly notes that

> If class depends on how people earn their living, that is on their occupations, changes in employment are bound to change the class structure. Old class formations have been undermined; this is beyond dispute, and is easily mistaken for a decline in class itself. Yet class inequalities (in market and work situations) remain very much alive. Indeed they are now wider than ever. (Roberts, 2001, p 80)

More recently Evans and Tilley have reinforced the continued relevance of this perspective (and the evidence presented in the previous chapter supports it) with their analysis of contemporary data. They argue that while working-class jobs may 'no longer be concentrated in traditional heavy manufacturing' (Evans and Tilley, 2017, p 4) the constraints and disadvantages associated with working-class employment (poor pay and a lack of other workplace benefits more commonly associated with middle-class jobs) remain very much alive. They argue that differences in the resources, prospects and security of the different classes remain as constant as, if not more pronounced today than they ever were (Evans and Tilley, 2017, p 4). While those at the very bottom of the class structure – most generally those experiencing or at greater risk of experiencing poverty – are generally shrinking in number, families who remain in this group 'for a second generation risk becoming detached from the rest of society' (Payne, 2017, p 166). Payne concludes that the lowest two social groups have shrunk from 31.7% to 24.1% of the labour force since the late 1990s yet their prospects are increasingly poor (Payne, 2017, p 166).

The Great British Class Survey published in 2015 has done something to put social class back on the popular agenda. The research has been very effective in highlighting not just the growing complexity in how we understand class in the contemporary context, but also the difficulties experienced by those at the bottom of the class structure. In their analysis the authors adopt the term 'precariat' (using it in a very different way to Standing, 2010) to describe those groups who are the 'missing people' (Savage, 2015, p 333), 'working in precarious jobs' and living precarious lives characterised by uncertainty and unstable and decaying environments (Savage, 2015, p 344). Savage (2015) also found that the prospects for those in the group that he chooses to call the 'precariat' were very bleak indeed. Thus, working-class life remains alive, if not always especially well, in the army of low-paid and insecure workers who keep Britain working, yet constitute a critical labour force which is largely hidden or, more often, simply ignored.

Poverty and the question of inheritance

Research has shown that the 'cultures of poverty' explanations of the problem resonate most with the general public (Scott-Paul, 2016), drawing on the age-old ideas of an undeserving underclass who are responsible for their own poverty. It is these ideas that continue to inform poverty propaganda in the current period. Welshman has shown how the infamous ideas of Sir Keith Joseph, who popularised the notion of 'cycles' of deprivation as a means of understanding why some families remained poor across generations, remain central to how poverty is largely presented and understood today. Joseph's ideas about the causes of working-age poverty were 'closely bound up with the concept of the problem family' and, as Welshman argues, 'he clearly regarded the low-paid and the unemployed – the able-bodied poor – as problems' (2007, p 77) who were generally deemed to be undererving and responsible for their own plight. These ideas remain central to the evolution of more recent discussions:

> Joseph's theme had been that of a hypothesis of a 'cycle of deprivation', whilst [Tony] Blair's was that of a new government's stance on social exclusion. But despite the passage of 34 years, the fact that one speech was given by a Conservative minister and the other by a Labour prime minister, and inevitable differences in language, the content

was remarkably similar. In all of the recent debate the rhetoric of a cycle of deprivation and of intergenerational continuities has been ever-present. (Welshman, 2013, p 2)

It is a simple but important fact that wealth tends to be perpetuated across generations within families, and the same is true of poverty (Hood and Joyce, 2017). Experiencing poverty in childhood tends to be closely correlated with a risk of experiencing poverty in later years. The notion that poverty is the responsibility – or fault – of the individuals who experience it is a stubborn idea that holds sway across all sectors of society, including among those experiencing poverty themselves (at least in respect of others' situations, if not their own) (Shildrick and MacDonald, 2013). The precise interaction between structural conditions and individual behaviours in explaining poverty is not necessarily easy to disentangle. As Blanden and Gibbons argue:

> It is extremely difficult to pin down the factors that *cause* the persistence of poverty. Income poverty goes hand-in-hand with numerous other forms of deprivation, some of which are consequences of the lack of resources in the household and others that lead to poverty in themselves. Many of these aspects of deprivation may be a result of other underlying factors that are very hard to measure and persist through individuals' lives. For all these reasons, it is extremely difficult to really understand the causal processes that lie at the root of the persistence of poverty through the lifecycle. (Blanden and Gibbons, 2006, p xi)

It is perhaps this wooliness or lack of clarity, that at least in part, helps to keep the individualised explanations of poverty alive. Of course, individual behaviours, experiences and life choices will always interact with the social and economic conditions that individuals face, and individuals will always have a greater or lesser degree of free choice and autonomy about what they choose to do or not to do. But it is also the case that experiencing poverty severely limits choices and restricts opportunities. While those experiencing poverty do as much as they can to navigate and mitigate these limits and restrictions, there is no getting away from the fact that having little money restricts life chances and serves to limit, constrain, oppress and dominate. Some do manage to overcome poverty and move away from the condition, and more research is needed around 'poverty escapes', but the reality for many people is that poverty is recurrent or lasting. The problems associated with poverty (of the sorts outlined in Chapter Three) are cumulative and by their very nature life-limiting and this in itself makes it harder to escape the condition.

Experiencing poverty not only makes it more likely that a person will face difficulties (whether those be around ill health, debts or other difficulties associated with living on a low or inadequate income) but it also means that the ability to mitigate or deal with such problems is seriously diminished. When Lord Freud, a prominent 'welfare' adviser and former investment banker made the comment that 'people who are poorer should be prepared to take the biggest risks; they have the least to lose' (Freud, 2012), he not only played into the generic poverty propaganda that is the focus of this book, reinforcing the supposed deficits of those experiencing poverty, but also completely misrepresented the realities of living on a low income.

For Biressi and Nunn social class is 'formed through material conditions' and, importantly, 'shaped by early disadvantage or natal privilege' (Biressi and Nunn, 2016, p 1). It is well documented that class inequalities start in the womb and continue to shape life chances through the life course. Townsend's interventions were crucial here in so far as he drew explicit attention to the range of resources needed to 'permit participation in the activities, customs and diets commonly approved by society' (Townsend, 1979, p 88) as having importance for the intergenerational continuity of poverty. Not only was Townsend 'the first to conceptualise poverty as relative' (Bradshaw, 2011, p 92), but he also drew attention to the importance of resources (such as housing, diet, access to leisure activities – and not just income) in understanding the experience of poverty. Importantly, he pointed to the structural causes of poverty and the importance of understanding 'class relations' (Townsend, 1979, pp 6–7) and the 'allocative principles and mechanisms and developments in the pattern of social life and consumption' (p 917).

A wealth of evidence has consistently illustrated that poverty in childhood has adverse effects on children's lives, affecting health, well-being and educational attainment (Ridge, 2002). Poverty and disadvantage limit life chances and opportunities. Evidence shows that these disadvantages have scarring effects into adulthood, making escape from poverty more difficult (Blanden and Gibbons, 2006). People experiencing poverty have little choice in terms of what foods they eat, they struggle to replace household items when they break and they are limited in giving their children Christmas and birthday treats. The notion that the playing field is level – and that opportunities are evenly distributed – is not only dishonest but helps to pave the way for poverty propaganda and associated narratives of the neoliberal aspirational self to flourish and thrive. Those experiencing poverty are depicted as lacking, whether that be in terms of work motivation, personal determination or intelligence, or all of these and more; importantly, this is framed in terms of personal deficits that are within the control of the individual. The role of financial (and other sorts of) capital in opening up opportunities and life chances – or, in the case of those experiencing poverty, closing them down – remains hidden. In a tightened economic climate inherited wealth (and associated opportunities) are becoming more important (Hood and Joyce, 2017). Quite simply this means that class privilege is becoming more entrenched, and that can only be bad news for those on low incomes who will find it ever harder to escape poverty. Hood and Joyce point out that:

> Today's elderly have much more wealth to bequeath than their predecessors, primarily as the result of rising homeownership rates and rising house prices. At the same time, today's young adults will find it harder to accumulate wealth of their own than previous generations did, due to the sharp fall in homeownership, the dramatic decline of defined benefit pensions in the private sector and the stagnation in household incomes. Together, these trends mean inherited wealth is likely to play a more important role in determining the lifetime economic resources of younger generations, with important implications for inequality and social mobility. (Hood and Joyce, 2017)

In such a context, class differences will inevitably become more pronounced as the struggle over resources and access to decent employment opportunities intensifies. As Ken Roberts has argued:

> As those from more affluent backgrounds see their middle class positions threatened, parents may be angered by the low salaries that their well-qualified children are being offered, the shortage of long-term career jobs and the debts that the young are incurring and frustrated that they, the elders, lack the resources to remedy or compensate for young people's difficulties. (Roberts, 2012, p 491)

What is important to bear in mind when thinking about inheritance and poverty, as well as wealth, is how the two are configured and presented and subsequently understood in the public and political imagination. Entitlement lies at the heart of this issue, where class positioning, whether for the more affluent or for those experiencing poverty, is presented as – and often largely understood to be – rightly and justly deserved.

This explicit framing of life chances is useful and convenient for those who have money, wealth and power. It is rather telling that in 2013 the then Prime Minister, David Cameron, was subjected to some awkward questioning after it emerged, partly via the Panama Paper leaks, that he had been given a £200,000 gift from his mother that was not subject to inheritance tax (Boffey, 2016). Amid questions around his father's off-shore investments, Cameron was subjected to uncomfortable questions about his own financial dealings. Yet what was interesting about this episode is that while the question (quite rightly) of how much tax had been paid or avoided was at the forefront of the issue (both in terms of how the media covered the issue and how it was debated by political figures and commentators), there was barely a mention of the £200,000 and coming on the back of another £300,000 that Cameron had inherited on his father's death a year earlier. It is a firmly British tradition – reinforced to the hilt in neoliberal regimes such as ours – that family wealth is deemed a private and personal matter, and that such wealth is earned and deserved. How such gains – that are often considerable, by most people's measures, as the above example illustrates – are come by is rarely even brought to the table for discussion.

It is the effects of inherited wealth and privilege (rather than the origins, which would require a much bigger conversation) that at least deserve to be acknowledged in debates about the causes and consequences of poverty. This is perhaps especially so in a context where the life chances of those experiencing poverty and other related disadvantages are perpetually dissected in ways that fail to acknowledge their unequal starting positions. The limits of poverty are assumed to be such that they can easily be overcome. The chances of any of the young people in our research studies in Teesside and Glasgow making it to Westminster, an institution that continues to be largely populated by elites, are slim at best, and more likely virtually non–existent (Bloodworth, 2016). David Cameron's journey to Westminster was made possible by his educational trajectory (including Eton College and Oxford University), which in turn was made possible by his family background and, in particular, familial wealth and privilege. So ingrained is the belief in deservingness in Britain (for both the rich and those who are economically disadvantaged) that the matters of inherited privilege and inherited disadvantage – and their role in subsequent life chances – are rarely questioned or laid bare. Research shows that the idea of 'just deserts', in terms of what people have and what they don't, is so deeply ingrained in the public psyche that the public are strongly in favour of scrapping inheritance tax (Whiting, 2016). It is to this idea of the 'Great Meritocracy' (May, 2017) that the chapter now turns.

The 'opportunity society' and the myth of meritocracy

Education is often held up as being the key that unlocks the door to upward social mobility, the so-called 'magic bullet' or 'great leveller' that allows those from less privileged backgrounds to work their way upwards and achieve a decent standard of living. Social mobility is where most of the political attention around poverty and disadvantage tends to be focused, with politician after politician offering to increase educational opportunities and close attainment gaps between disadvantaged children and the rest. Typical sentiments expressed by politicians of all stripes tend to posit that social mobility is a desirable thing and that there is not enough of it in British society:

> A key aim of this government's 'one nation' ideal is to tackle the root causes of our unequal society – to support families, to improve education, to give people the help they need to get into work. This is the best way to improve life chances for all. We are determined to ensure that educational excellence is available to every single child and young person, everywhere in this country. To raise the bar and heighten expectations, and to give schools and colleges the support they need to meet them ...//... Under our reforms, stronger schools will flourish, sharing best practice and innovation, and weaker schools will be identified and turned around quickly. To deliver real social justice and ensure every child can go to a great school regardless of background or where he or she lives, we need to ensure consistent, world-class teaching across the country. (DfE, 2016, pp 3–4)

Theresa May has echoed similar sentiments in recent times, arguing that she is determined to break down the barriers that prevent people from poorer backgrounds from achieving their potential (May 2016), and the Conservatives' 2017 election manifesto resurrected the idea of the Great Meritocracy. May, as Prime Minister, has been very vocal in declaring her determination to offer opportunities to those who are disadvantaged. It is worth quoting at some length from the speech that she made on taking office.

> "We will fight against the burning injustice that, if you're born poor, you will die on average 9 years earlier than others. If you're black, you're treated more harshly by the criminal justice system than if you're white. If you're a white, working-class boy, you're less likely than anybody else in Britain to go to university. If you're at a state school, you're less likely to reach the top professions than if you're educated privately ...//... But the mission to make Britain a country that works for everyone means more than fighting these injustices. If you're from an ordinary working class family, life is much harder than many people in Westminster realize. You have a job but you don't always have job security. You have your own home, but you worry about paying a mortgage. You can just about manage but you worry about the cost of living and getting your kids into a good school. If you're one of those families, if you're just managing, I want to address you directly. I know you're working around the clock, I know you're doing your best, and I know that sometimes life can be a struggle. The government I lead will be driven not by the interests of the privileged few, but by yours. We will do everything we can to give you more control over your lives. When we take the big calls, we'll think *not of the powerful, but you*. When we pass new laws, *we'll listen not to the mighty, but to you*. When it comes to taxes, *we'll prioritize not the wealthy, but you*. When it comes to opportunity, *we won't entrench the advantages of the fortunate few*. We will do everything we can to help anybody, whatever your background, to go as far as your talents will take you." (May, 2016)

These are important words that support and cement the broader poverty propaganda that cites individual failings as being key causes of poverty. The framing of the problems as not being explicitly about individual behaviour, aspiration or motivation, and with a direct implication that there are structural barriers that lie beyond the individual, is very important. Mrs May's words were carefully crafted to engender a perception that she, as the leader of a newly formed government, had empathy and sympathy as well as understanding for the plight of the less fortunate. This is really important, as evidence shows that those who are experiencing poverty and related lack of opportunities are rarely oblivious to the unfairness of their situations. It is unlikely that May had had a complete change of political heart when she spoke these words; she had, after all, been a key player in a government that had systematically undermined and dismantled opportunities for the least economically well-off in society, as has been detailed in the pages of this book. It is perhaps rather telling that the Social Mobility Commission, set up by the Coalition in 2011 to try and address these pressing questions, has a rather uncertain future as the Chair, Sir Alan Milburn, and several other committee members resigned their roles in December 2017. In his resignation letter, Milburn said:

> I have little hope of the current government making the progress I believe is necessary to bring about a fairer Britain. It seems unable to commit to the future of the Commission as an independent body or to give due priority to the social mobility challenge facing our nation. (Milburn, 2017)

The sentiments crafted above by Theresa May are pretty typical of those that stoke the fires of poverty propaganda and are also indicative of the gulf between rhetoric and reality. It is likely, too, that Theresa May would also, at the time of speaking, have been mindful of the emerging undercurrent of anger felt by those who for decades have been largely excluded from the benefits of neoliberal capitalism and which seemed to have come to the fore at the time of the vote to leave the European Union. Cleverly, and perhaps not by chance, May's words reinforce the widely accepted division between the supposed deserving and undeserving. She appeals directly to those 'hard working families', set apart from the supposedly work-shy and feckless, and of course in doing so she appeals to the majority of the population (from those experiencing poverty to those on average and middling incomes) who all, in one way or another, perceive themselves to be 'ordinary', 'hard-working' and 'normal' (Savage et al, 2001).

Credential inflation means that education is necessary for even relatively low-skilled and low-paid jobs. Young people are expected to remain in education for longer; the opportunities to take advantage of higher education have increased, with more working-class entrants gaining higher-level qualifications than in the past. The increasing numbers of working-class graduates and first-generation graduates in families have also added to the growth of what I call the messy middle. Yet evidence shows that sharp class distinctions remain in educational outcomes. As Harris and Ranson argue, the bond between social class and education is a particularly 'powerful and resistant one' (Harris and Ranson, 2005, p 571). Despite numerous policy initiatives aimed at overcoming these inequalities, from the introduction of comprehensive schooling in the 1960s to the current ambitions of the Conservative government around grammar schools, stubborn inequalities in educational outcomes by class remain, and in the current economic and social climate they appear, predictably, to be worsening. Educational qualifications tend to be related to job outcomes (although not completely straightforwardly) but, as we will see below, these educational and employment trajectories remain strongly predictable by social class, particularly at the upper and lower levels of the labour market (Gallie, 2015). It is no accident that 'poor work' tends to be by and large dominated by people from lower social-class backgrounds, for whom such jobs are rarely a stepping-stone to something better (Shildrick et al, 2012a).

In our research young people generally left school with few qualifications, and this restricted the sorts of jobs that they were able to access. It is well accepted that children from working-class backgrounds continue to perform less well in education than their better-off peers, and this fact has remained a historical constant since the inception of the education system as we know it 1944 (Crawford et al, 2014). Crawford et al tracked the educational trajectories of high-achieving children from low-income backgrounds. They point out that not only are children from poorer backgrounds less likely to do well but, from the small numbers that start on a high-achieving trajectory, many will fall back. They point out that

> Children who are high attaining at age 7 are more likely to fall off a high attainment trajectory than children from richer backgrounds. We find that high achieving children from the most deprived families perform worse than lower achieving students from the least deprived families at Key Stage 4. (Crawford et al, 2014, p 8)

Diane Reay's work has been instrumental in highlighting the inherent difficulties that working-class young people face in educational settings, illustrating how the school has become a site of 'working class educational failure' (Reay, 1998, p 1). Her work shows how 'Black and white working class mothers were working just as hard on their children's educational attainment as white, middle class mothers ...//... but it was not hard work that counted' (Reay, 1998, p 1).

What did in fact count was that education (as with other institutions and social structures) is 'geared to unequal outcomes' (Reay, 1998, p 3). Kirby (2016) highlights the importance of extra home tuition in facilitating social mobility. This aspect of education is described as a 'hidden secret', largely neglected in conversations about schooling and disproportionately delivered to children who are already advantaged (Kirby, 2016). Gillies (2005) has also illustrated how classed values and opportunities impact on the ways in which families are able to engage with education. Her research has illuminated the extent to which 'economic, cultural, social and personal resources are interdependent' (Gillies, 2005, p 842). She has aptly illustrated how 'Parents with access to middle class resources (such as money, high status social contacts and legitimated cultural knowledge) drew on these capitals to consolidate their power and advantage, and invested heavily in their children's education as a method of transferring privilege' (Gillies, 2005, p 842); and, conversely, that 'working class parents were more concerned to ensure their children have the skills and the strength to be able to cope with the instability, injustice and hardship that will most likely characterise their lives' (p 842).

It is the ability to take advantage of an education system that has become increasingly marketised that allows middle-class parents to engage in the right sort of 'class work' to ensure that their children benefit from the best education possible (Devine, 2004). Wider inequalities that impact on how parents are able to engage include their own educational backgrounds and unequal gender relations. The educational trajectories of the working-class women in Reay's research were important in understanding how the women interacted with and related to their children's schools. Devine's research has also been very important in showing how middle-class parents use their own histories, resources and personal contacts to help maintain their own educational positions and achievements. Her work in Britain and the US illustrated the ways in which middle-class parents 'mobilised their economic resources to secure their children's educational and occupational success' (Devine, 2004, p 42). Devine argues that in tightened economic conditions these class practices will become more important for middle-class parents, who may themselves have enjoyed a level of upward mobility and wish to retain the best possible outcomes for their own children. Blanden and Gibbons point to the importance of historical conditions across generations as their work shows that

> Poverty from the teens into the early thirties has risen over time, with teenage poverty having a greater impact on

later outcomes for teenagers in the 1980s compared with teenagers in the 1970s. This finding adds to the wider evidence that family background has had a growing impact on later outcomes between these cohorts. (Blanden and Gibbons, 2006)

A House of Lords report on social mobility has argued that young people are being let down by a system that serves those who are already advantaged and leaves behind those who are already being underserved (House of Lords, 2016). Private education plays an important role in perpetuating an intergenerational privileged elite in Britain and thus leading to virtual social closure in respect of the top professions. As Bloodworth points out:

> A glance at the country's professions betrays a country dominated by an affluent elite. Just 7 per cent of Britons are privately educated, yet according to a government report published in 2014, 33 per cent of MPs, 71 per cent of senior judges and 44 per cent of people in *The Sunday Times Rich List* attended fee paying schools. Almost half of newspaper columnists and a quarter of BBC executives were also products of the private school system. (Bloodworth, 2016, pp 51–2)

Westminster and politics in general tends to be dominated by those who have been privately educated. It is no coincidence that Parliament is saturated by those with a private education, a significant number of our prime ministers having been educated at prestigious fee-paying schools such as Harrow, Eton or the elite Westminster School that overlooks Parliament and Westminster Abbey (and charges over £30,000 a year in school fees alone, before the additional expenses of uniforms, sports equipment and school trips). In 2012 the Labour MP Denis MacShane argued that 'all working class' shortlists should be introduced in 10% of parliamentary seats to make the House of Commons more representative of the public it represents (Wheeler, 2012). Heath has shown how the number of MPs from manual working-class backgrounds has declined significantly, from 20% in 1964 to just 5% by 2010 (Heath, 2015). Not only might it be more 'credible when a politician from a working-class background says that they will stand up for the underprivileged, than when a multi-millionaire member of the aristocracy says the same thing' (Heath, 2015); it is also the case that such individuals may have a better, closer understanding of the realities of the issues that the underprivileged face. As Payne rightly notes:

> To the extent that elites share a privileged background, they consequently have less first hand experience of going to ordinary state schools or the home life of other classes. This limits their personal knowledge and reduces their capacity to empathise with less fortunate people. (Payne, 2017, p 162)

This issue was brought into sharp relief when, shortly after the 2010 election, it was observed that the Coalition cabinet was composed almost entirely of millionaires (Heath, 2015).

Furthermore, it is increasingly the case that the graduate labour market is stratified along classed lines and evidence suggests that these divisions are becoming more entrenched. A report by the Higher Education Funding Council for England (HEFCE) noted that 'Graduates from the most advantaged backgrounds (based on the Participation of Local Areas 3 measure of young participation in higher education) have substantially higher professional employment rates than those from the least advantaged backgrounds, at both six and 40 months after qualifying, for both cohorts' (HEFCE, 2016). Indeed, getting a degree from a Russell Group institution is fast becoming a key marker of inequality between graduates, and that which affords access to the higher-level professions (Savage, 2015; Payne, 2017). Higher education has opened its doors to people from less privileged class backgrounds and has proved to be an important mechanism whereby those who have failed in – and been failed by – their earlier educational experiences can re-engage. Yet, research shows that the difficulties of living in poverty and of struggling in low-paid employment are serious barriers to re-engaging in education (Shildrick et al, 2012a). When people are experiencing poverty the sheer hardships and complexities of life and work can make it incredibly difficult to re-engage, even where there is a will to do so. Education is also expensive and may be simply out of the question for people on limited budgets.

The general idea that we live in a meritocracy has become reasonably well embedded in the public psyche since the 1970s. Essentially, the British equivalent of the American dream tends to hold much power with the British public; thus, the inequalities of opportunity, which are so crucial for people experiencing poverty, tend to recede in visibility and importance. The language of the meritocratic society shifts according to the political climate of the day, but the general message does not fundamentally change. From the 'classless society' of

John Major (Prime Minister 1990–97) to 'the opportunity society' of Tony Blair (Prime Minister 1997–2007), now, under Prime Minister Theresa May, the language has shifted to being about 'ending burning injustice for the white working class and ethnic minorities' (May, 2016) and the desire for a Great Meritocracy. The shift towards individualised ways of thinking about and structuring the social world, underpinned by the idea that anyone can be anyone if they really try, came to the fore during the Thatcher government of the 1980s; indeed Margaret Thatcher was fond of referring to herself as the daughter of a grocer, to explicitly reinforce the idea that upward social mobility and high office was a route open to all. It is an idea that has longevity and widespread popular appeal. Thatcher was raised in Grantham, 'the epitome of middle England', received 'piano lessons' and made 'compulsory library visits'. According to her biographer Hugo Young, she was 'born to be a politician', raised in a political family who 'handed down the tradition of political commitment from one generation to the next' (Young, 1989, p 3). It is probably safe to say that Thatcher's life story would have almost certainly have been a very different one had she started life, like our research participants and many others similar to them, in disadvantaged circumstances and in depressed and deprived localities where local libraries are either under threat of closure or have in many cases already closed, and where piano lessons, or for that matter paid-for hobbies of any sort, are for many quite simply out of the question. In our research projects it was frequently the aspiration for a holiday that came through in many of our interviewees' accounts of what they felt they might be missing out on when living with poverty. Our interviewees rarely went away on holiday and mostly refused to take out expensive debt in order to so, but the aspiration to take a holiday was deeply embedded in their minds as a key symbol of what it might be like not to live in poverty (Shildrick et al, 2012a).

There are a number of problems with the idea of social mobility as a route away from poverty. First, routes to the best-paid occupations tend to be secured via a successful educational background and we have seen in this section how the odds of educational achievement are stacked very firmly against those who experience poverty. We also know that routes into professional jobs are heavily determined by not just educational achievements but also social networks (as is entry into jobs at most levels of the labour market); hence, even when people from disadvantaged backgrounds manage to accrue the necessary qualifications to enter, say, medicine or the law, they often still lack the right sort of extra-curricular activities (in the form of hobbies or gap-year activities) as well as the contacts and networks that would help in accessing these sorts of jobs. A key issue that the House of Lords report points to is the importance of social networks in getting work:

> Employer recruitment practices disadvantage those in the middle and at the bottom end of the labour market. Small and medium-sized businesses in particular rely on informal means of recruitment, such as word-of-mouth. Using this sort of recruitment means that applicants' existing social connections and networks are important and lead to their success. Not all young people will have these connections. We welcome the fact that some employers are already changing their recruitment practices to address these problems. We note however that these changes are not widespread, are limited to the largest employers and will not go far enough on their own to achieve real progress. (House of Lords Select Committee on Social Mobility, 2016, p 6)

Gaffney and Baumberg argue that 'the chance members of a given generation will move into a different social class from their parents has changed very little since the middle of the last century' (Gaffney and Baumberg, 2015, p 6). If you start at the bottom, evidence shows you probably won't venture far from it. The problems of social class immobility are heightened and exacerbated in the current context, where young people are being particularly adversely affected both by the global recession and by the austerity and other policy measures that have been implemented since 2010. Savage (2015) has shed light on this issue, describing the class structure as equivalent to a mountain: some groups starting near to the top find it altogether easier to retain their hold at the top, while those at the bottom quite literally have a mountain to climb to make it all the way to the top or even part way up. The analogy is useful, as it also points to the ways in which those at the top not only access the top much more easily but also occupy a finite number of positions at the top, such that there are fewer positions left for those lower down the mountain to access, regardless of personal motivation or determination to do so. As Savage points out, 'few of those on the mountain tops, or even the valley sides, move down. It is actually rather difficult to fall all the way down the mountain slopes!' (Savage, 2015, p 193). The sorts of low-paid jobs that trap people in poverty are generally undertaken by people similar to those who have been interviewed across our research studies (Shildrick et al, 2012a), and who have generally not been served well by the state education system. Our interviewees were restricted in next steps by geographical factors. They often had numerous home responsibilities that impacted on their ability to take paid work and to travel to work. Low-paid jobs do not afford the luxury of travelling particularly far, and it was of little surprise that the sorts of jobs our interviewees did were ones that they found they could afford or manage to travel to. Interestingly, this was something that employers whom we talked to (Shildrick et al, 2012a) also sometimes referred to as being their preference for taking employees into low-paid work. A care home manager told us how they actively sought employees in the local area as they felt they were more likely to be reliable and to turn up to work on time (Shildrick et al, 2012a). Amanda (aged 50) told us of her experiences walking some distance to take up work in a well-known take-away restaurant after many years of difficulties in her life and being unable to work (Shildrick et al, 2010, 2012a). Her insights are useful not just in terms of her experiences of getting from where she lived to the workplace but in terms of the multitude of challenges and disadvantages that overlay attempts to find work. She also offers some insight into what it can be like to undertake 'poor work':

"How I got to that, I was freezing, freezing literally, the gas had gone out again, you cannot survive if you are a single person. Nobody's helping you what-so-ever, you're putting your money in the gas meter and your electric you're paying the water, you're paying your TV, you're paying, if you've got five pound to put on your mobile phone, it's cheaper than using the phone box. Bus fares. They're very expensive. Then you've got your wash powder, deodorant, shampoo. They're all luxuries. They are now. Um yeah, and then you're buying a newspaper instead of walking three miles to the library to look for jobs. So yeah, I couldn't afford that. Um, and I was totally frustrated at the fact I was freezing and I couldn't see why me money wasn't stretching because basically it doesn't. [At the time she was getting £64 JSA] ... and then I was scared that if I went to work I wouldn't get my rent paid. That is a scary thing for a lot of people. You know, and you're going to be homeless, you've already lost your kids you've got nowt to eat, you're freezing anyway, you know, are you gonna risk it? ...//... So I went to the Job Centre and I thought right, that's it I'm determined now, you've got to have a determination, I'm going to get any job I don't care what it is ... famous last words, oh, I don't care what it is [*laughs*]. I'm not going to say that again."

Eventually Amanda was offered a job at the take-away, and she went on to describe her experiences. She had experienced a successive range of problems and issues throughout her life and was returning to work after a relatively long period out of work and having suffered serious depression and related problems. All of her children had been taken into care after her own troubled childhood spilled over into her adult life and affected her ability to care for them as she progressed through a series of highly abusive relationships with the children's fathers. Her experiences at the take-away restaurant were reported to us as follows:

> "It wasn't very satisfactory but I got the job. You're working and working and working, and you're working. And there's no days off and your wages are obviously projecting how many days you're working. £5.80 an hour. Eight and a half hours a day, eight days solid. And you literally, you get ten minutes' break in the afternoon if you're lucky. And they scream at you negatively all the time, you're not allowed to stand still and the sweat is dripping off you. ... I'm supposed to be the girl who cleans the tables, so I was doing upstairs, downstairs, doing the books, doing the staff books, doing all the building. And emptying all those great big bins, you have to pull them, that's why me shoulder's gone. Flinging them in and out, taking them outside in the snow this deep. You're just ... numb. Actually it was awful and you end up crying, or skitting out, like they all do in that job. But then I thought well at least its paying the rent and I'm doing it meself. And then January came, and obviously trade goes. So it's sort of, we don't need you here today, we don't need you there today, we've cut your hours, and you're scrimping to pay the rent. And the council tax, and the water, and the telly, and the TV, and the telephone, and the gas and the electric, and the bus fares, so you start walking to work. Three-quarters of an hour there, three-quarters of an hour back, after you've done eight and a half hours of solid labour as I call it. You get the abuse off the customers, you get the daft drunk young 14-year-olds, upstairs flinging things at you and swearing. You get taking drugs in the toilets so you gotta sort that. I'm cleaning toilets at [...]. In the end I got ill. My back literally, went. This horrendous horrible

pain and I couldn't walk or sit, and it went up my arm, and I was getting these horrible headaches. You literally cannot stay still otherwise you're screamed at ..."

Poor work is undertaken by the working-class, not the upper- or middle-class for the most part. That David Cameron ended up in Westminster rather than a well-known burger take-away, a care home or a warehouse was no accident. Personal drive and motivation may take people so far, but it rarely promotes them from the bottom to the top. It is not just educational achievements in and of themselves that serve to perpetuate these patterns of class inequality. As Payne points out, 'private schools and Russell Group universities combined with forms of familial cultural advantage offer a separate route to the best jobs, such as the old professions' (Payne, 2017, p 161). The old adage that it is not what you know but who you know holds as much value in terms of accounting for who gets what in the jobs market as it ever did. A further problem with the issue of social mobility and the notion that it offers a pathway away from poverty is the fact that there are a limited number of positions in society that attract good levels of pay and working conditions (of the sort we read about in Chapter Four). Importantly, and in many cases, vital jobs do not allow people to move away from poverty; instead, they support and perpetuate the condition in contemporary Britain. The relative value attached to jobs in Britain, as symbolised by pay and conditions, is grossly unequal. As we saw earlier in this chapter pathways towards different jobs are largely determined by social-class origins (and this will be perhaps even more so as we move forward in a tightened economic climate). We might also usefully ask what value we attribute as a society to important jobs that are often insecure and low paid. Care work might be a case in point. Skeggs recently wrote movingly of her struggles to get her parents cared for in their old age and as their health declined. She writes of the carers:

It's also hard to experience first-hand the levels of exploitation of the carers. Even though I was paying £17.90 per hour, they receive less than £10, and the sheer resentment towards their agency as a result of their working conditions: zero hours, minimal training, no time to travel, monitoring, dodgy tax scheme, and being treated without respect, is affectively contagious. (Skeggs, 2017)

In contrast to other writers, Payne argues that social mobility rates in the UK are actually relatively high. For Payne, it is the underlying inequalities (and inequalities of opportunity) that make up a significant part of the problem. He argues that 'the silver bullet of social mobility will not kill social inequalities' (Payne, 2017, p 169). He goes on to suggest that 'improving mobility rates will do little to reduce social inequality, but reducing social inequality is the sure way to achieving greater social mobility' (Payne, 2017, p 173). That privilege and prosperity more often pave the way to elite professions rather than toiling away in a low-paid, insecure job in a nursing home or in a warehouse is of perhaps little surprise, but the deceit of the situation is to pretend that these factors do not matter.

Conclusion

Erik Olin Wright argues that

> Class remains a significant and sometimes powerful determinant of many aspects of social life. Class boundaries, especially the property boundary, continue to constitute real barriers in people's lives; inequalities in the distribution of capital assets continue to have real consequences for material interests; capitalist firms continue to face the problem of extracting labour effort from non-owning employees; and class location continues to have a real, if variable, impact on individual subjectivities. (Wright, E.O., 2015, p 155)

Social class is integral to understanding poverty in Britain today but it tends to be marginal, if not completely absent, in most discussions of the topic. Rather, the discussion of poverty is often hidden behind other terminology, such as social exclusion, economic marginality and social and economic disadvantage. In some respects the failure to call out poverty for what it is relates to the difficulties of challenging the condition and addressing it (we return to this issue in Chapter Eight). The individualisation of class (and other elements of social life) has played an important role in diminishing social class as an obvious marker of inequality. With colleagues, in an earlier book, we wrote of the 'great myth and the great illogic' (Shildrick et al, 2012, p 221) about the ways in which the unemployed have been consistently described as 'scroungers' as a precursor to increasingly punitive 'welfare' reforms and sanctions – and when there are simply not enough jobs to satisfy demand. We argued then that myths usually have a purpose.

'They distract attention, cover up realities and justify actions' (p 223). The myth of the classless society and the myths of social mobility and meritocracy operate in similar ways, to conceal and to distract attention from the realities of class inequality. They work in tandem with pernicious myths about 'welfare'. Processes of individualisation heighten the power of these ideas, adding weight to the notion that those experiencing poverty need to change – to become more aspirational, more ambitious, less complacent and lazy – and, most importantly, that the power to change their lives for the better lies within individuals. These myths obscure the fact that social mobility is limited and that the odds are very firmly stacked against those at the bottom of the economic pile. Through nothing but an accident of birth, the children born into the poorest circumstances have little chance of climbing up the greasy pole of employment or reaching anywhere higher than the lower slopes of the mountain (to borrow Savage's analogy). The weight of social class brings with it constraints and limits for those on low incomes. These constraints and limits are not immutable, nor are they impossible to overcome, but they exist, they are real and they need to be acknowledged.

SIX

Poverty: discrimination, stigma and shame

Introduction

> Shame is taken to be externally imposed by society, via individuals and through social institutions, but internalized and experienced as a powerful negative emotion that results in social withdrawal and powerlessness. (Walker, 2014, p 2)

> "They are making people feel like they are not up to scratch. Stop putting out that propaganda about scroungers. Stop trying to put fear into an already unsteady person. Stop trying to drive people by fear. You are a valuable piece of society." (Amanda, aged 50, Teesside interviewee in Shildrick et al, 2012b)

> "When I go to my constituency, in fact when I walk around, you can almost now tell somebody's background by their weight ...//... Obviously not everyone who is overweight comes from deprived backgrounds, but that's where the propensity lies." (Anna Soubry, MP, 2013)

This chapter develops the material in the previous chapter by looking at the concepts of stigma and shame. Central to understanding the issue of shame is the concept of 'respectability', which Skeggs (1997) powerfully argues is one of the most 'ubiquitous signifiers of class' (p 1) and which constitutes both a 'marker and a burden of class' (p 3). The ideas of shame and respectability have long been central to narratives about poverty and provided the foundation of notions about the 'undeserving poor', and they provide a really important mechanism that allows poverty propaganda to work. At one and the same time shame is both a cause and a consequence of poverty propaganda. People in poverty strongly buy into dominant narratives about the supposed feckless behaviour of people experiencing poverty – at least as applying to others – and this allows poverty propaganda to work to garner consent for policies that penalise, stigmatise and deepen poverty for those on low incomes (Shildrick and MacDonald, 2013).

Poverty: stigma and shame

That shame is associated with poverty is nothing new, but the increasing emphasis on conspicuous consumption and focus on individual responsibility, aspiration and achievement really throw this issue into sharp relief as it becomes ever more clear that poverty has not just material and physical effects but psychosocial ones too (Lister, 2004; Baumberg et al, 2012; Walker, 2014; Walker and Chase, 2015). As Walker points out, it is important to take seriously 'the psychosocial dimensions of poverty and in particular the contention that there is a universal and immutable link between poverty and shame' (Walker, 2014, p 1). In a significant and ground-breaking piece of research Walker and colleagues have shown how shame is at the 'absolutist core' of the experience of poverty (Walker et al, 2013, p 215). Having undertaken qualitative research in seven countries (Uganda, India, China, Pakistan, South Korea, Finland and the UK) they argue that

> Accounts of the lived experience of poverty were found to be very similar, despite massive disparities in material circumstances associated with locally defined poverty lines, suggesting that relative notions of poverty are an appropriate basis for international comparisons. Though socially and culturally nuanced, shame was found to be associated with poverty in each location, variably leading to pretence, withdrawal, self-loathing, 'othering', despair, depression, thoughts of suicide and generally to reductions in personal efficacy. While internally felt, poverty-related shame was equally imposed by the attitudes and behaviour of those not in poverty, framed by public discourse and influenced by the objectives and implementation of anti-poverty policy. The evidence appears to confirm the negative consequences of shame, implicates it as a factor in increasing the persistence of poverty and suggests important implications for the framing, design and delivery of anti-poverty policies. (Walker et al, 2013, pp 215–16)

Shame is important because, according to Walker and colleagues, it is 'one of the most pernicious of emotions creating a sense of powerlessness and incompetence' (Walker et al, 2013, p 217). It is also about a feeling of failure and lack and can invoke behaviours to try to reduce the stigma or to appear to conform to the ubiquitous middle-class norm that we discussed in the previous chapter. Feelings of anger, distress and frustration are also increasingly recognised to be important, as people who experience poverty are not unaware of the injustices and unfairness of their situations, but these all too often are internalised and understood in individualised ways. What is so valuable about Walker and colleagues' work is that their study was able to look internationally and show how, while experiences of poverty varied, it was the fundamental shaming elements that remained constant. The research points to the importance of 'keeping up appearances' (Walker et al, 2013, p 123): in their different ways and across different countries respondents sought to appear 'normal' and 'respectable' (p 123). These pressures were often manifest through children, in so far as people were keen to ensure that their children looked clean and tidy (Uganda) or did not stand out from the rest (Oslo). The research found that

> Keeping up appearances could and frequently did lead respondents into a charade in which they concealed problems, pretended things were fine and avoided situations in which their circumstances and their shame could be exposed. (Walker et al, 2013, p 123)

Of course, this trying to hold things together has physical as well as emotional effects, and we saw earlier in the book how ill health is a common consequence of living with poverty. In Walker and colleagues' work the fear of shaming led respondents to withdraw from certain activities. Invitations to weddings, receptions and other events were often declined. It has long been known that living in poverty curtails social life (Shildrick et al, 2012a) because, quite simply, if you have little money you can't afford social or leisure activities. Yet, what is interesting about Walker and colleagues' research is the ways in which the economic effects of poverty interact with the emotional. Declining social opportunities because of fear about how one will be perceived, or because one may suffer stress and anxiety about having to reciprocate in some way, add a critical new dimension to understanding the effects of poverty and, in particular, 'the corrosive effects of poverty-related shame' (Walker et al, 2013, p 125).

Some years ago Sennett and Cobb (1972) wrote about the hidden injuries of class as a way of understanding how class is not just a matter of money but also one of feelings. They point to the 'corrosive power of the great American dream of dignity through upward mobility' (p 169). They also point out that

> Dignity is as compelling a human need as food or sex, and yet, here is a society which casts the mass of its people into limbo, never satisfying their hunger for dignity, nor yet so explicitly depriving them that the task of proving dignity seems an unreasonable burden, and revolt against society the only reasonable alternative. (Sennett and Cobb, 1972, p 191)

Research has shown that people often feel shame in terms of, for example, having to claim out-of-work benefits. This is not just because of the difficulties that people regularly report in negotiating the complexities of the system, but because it provokes a feeling of shame that they are unable provide for themselves and their families. Baumberg et al (2012) have shown how people experiencing poverty can feel shame in respect of claiming benefits because they believe that it may be perceived by others as a personal failure:

> We suggest that benefit stigma can operate on three levels, personal, social, and institutional, although these interact. Our survey found that personal stigma was restricted to a minority, social stigma is quite common, and that institutional stigma is widespread. Benefit stigma in Britain is primarily driven by the perception that claimants are 'undeserving'. Key criteria for achieving a 'deserving' status were need, and the level of responsibility that claimants were seen to hold for their own situation. (Baumberg et al, 2012, p 3)

That people should feel shame in claiming out of work benefits is perhaps of little surprise, given the poverty propaganda we read about in Chapter Two. Worries and concerns about how others might perceive their lives and situations are a common theme in research with people experiencing poverty. This can sometimes lead to anger and frustration, as people feel the injustice of being judged in a way that bears little relationship to the reality of their lives or situations. Research by Reutter and colleagues in Canada found the same. Their research revealed that stigmatising narratives are deeply felt. Interviewees related overwhelmingly negative accounts of how they felt labelled, judged and stereotyped by others.

> Our findings pertaining to perceptions of social identity suggest that participants living in poverty generally have a strong sense of stigma consciousness – a belief that they are viewed negatively, as a burden to society and essentially undeserving of what they get. (Reutter et al, 2009, p 302)

Reutter et al's interviewees were not just passive recipients but were also often aware of the unfairness of judgements that reflected little of the realities of their lives. Anger and an acute awareness of the injustice of stereotypes was something that sometimes came through in my own research, and Ruth Patrick found something very similar in her work with people claiming 'welfare' (Patrick, 2017). In our Teesside projects it was this shame at claiming benefits that, in part, drove interviewees' commitment to low-paid, poor work (Shildrick et al, 2010; 2012a). In Ruetter and colleagues' work, respondents reported how they occasionally challenged small examples of unfair treatment and then felt that they were alternatively stereotyped and labelled as 'having an attitude' or 'being difficult' (Reutter et al, 2009, p 304). We see below how the behaviour of agencies in respect of those who experience poverty is often informed by stigmatising labels and stereotypes of the sort that make up the poverty propaganda that is the main subject of this book. Importantly, those people are the very ones who have significant power over people experiencing poverty, making judgements about them, their lives and what they may – or may not – be entitled to.

Shame and stigma associated with poverty are intertwined with and overlaid by broader class stigmatisation. Skeggs' work has illustrated how working-class women try to avoid the stigma associated with being working class. She notes that

> Immersed in the lives and spaces of a group of white working-class women over time I became highly conscious of the numerous ways in which they were constantly subject to negative value judgements about their futures and pasts, behaviour, intelligence, taste, bodies and sexuality, to such an extent that it shaped their spatial sense of entitlement, engagement and limit: where they did or did not want to go, how they felt they could or could not 'be'. 'Being looked down on' was their description of a process to which they were continually subject, a visual assessment by others that repeatedly positioned them as lacking value. For instance, when they entered 'posh shops' they were acutely aware

of the way they were being read and judged by others.
(Skeggs, 2010, p 348)

A project undertaken by ATD Fourth World found that 'stigmatization was a recurrent theme during the research. Participants recounted how they were labelled as liars, unclean, feckless and lazy, often insulted by officials, and blamed for not accessing development programmes'. (ATD Fourth World, 2013, p 17). The research, assessing the Millennium Development Goals, was undertaken with 12 different countries, yet the experiences of stigmatisation were found to be remarkably consistent, just as in the research by Walker and colleagues. For Lister, this stigmatisation is a processes of 'othering' whereby those experiencing poverty are portrayed as distinct and different from the majority. Thus:

> The notion of 'the poor' as Other is used here to signify the many ways in which 'the poor' are treated as different from the rest of society. The capital 'O' denotes its symbolic weight. The notion of *Othering* conveys how this is not an inherent state but an on-going process animated by the 'non-poor'. It is a dualistic process of differentiation and demarcation by which the line is drawn between 'us' and 'them' – between the more and the less powerful – and through which social distance is established and maintained.
> (Lister, 2004, p 101)

Research shows very clearly that these are not just discourses that are passed downwards from the powerful and onto those experiencing poverty. People experiencing poverty draw on widespread and powerful discourses about poverty and the undeserving poor to try to distinguish their own experiences of poverty from those of others (Shildrick and MacDonald, 2013). For Lister, it is the case that 'the significance of stigma and shame is not to be underestimated. They play an important role in maintaining inequality and social hierarchy' (Lister, 2004, p 113).

Working-class consumption, the problems of excess and the emergence of the 'poor' consumer

Consumer behaviour has become an increasingly important marker of inequality and social class in the current context. As Shavitt and colleagues argue,

> Consumer behaviour could hardly be understood without considering social class. Our position in the social hierarchy has a powerful influence on almost everything in our daily lives – where we live, what we wear, where we travel, dine and shop, what we drive, and what media we consume. (Shavitt et al, 2016, p 583)

Consumption is important not just because it is ubiquitous and an integral and important part of contemporary society but also because it provides one of the key mechanisms that supports the middle-class norm that we read about in the last chapter. Markers of respectability are increasingly, if not almost wholly, bound up with heavily promoted and marketed appropriate or desirable consumption behaviours that have become key markers of class and inequality. People experiencing poverty find themselves in positions that are increasingly hard to navigate. They lack the financial capabilities to make open, individually determined choices in respect of what and how they consume. We discussed in Chapter Three the challenges of day-to-day living and the restriction of choice that this entails when one is living with very limited financial resources. People experiencing poverty are severely restricted in what they are able to consume but face the onslaught of pressure to achieve some level of middle-class respectable consumption the same as others with more resources. Hence those experiencing poverty are positioned in popular and political discourse as 'flawed consumers', either for their lack of ability to consume in supposedly socially acceptable ways or simply because their consumption practices are deemed inappropriate (Hamilton, 2012). As Bauman notes, 'if "being poor" once derived its meaning from the condition of being unemployed, today it draws its meaning primarily from the plight of a flawed consumer' (Bauman, 1998, p 1). It is through the consumption 'choices' of those experiencing poverty that an overt process of stigmatisation occurs. The poor are deemed to be 'defective consumers' (Bauman, 2013, p 61), whose 'non-shopping is the jarring and festering stigma of a life unfulfilled, a mark of nonentity and good-for-nothingness' (Bauman, 2013, p 61) which denigrates their value and their worth. Consumer behaviour in groups with limited incomes is also very explicitly positioned in popular and political discourse as evidence of not just their lack of taste but also their rejection of widespread middle-class respectability norms.

The supposed deficits inherent in the consumption habits and practices of those experiencing poverty are also held up as evidence that people cannot be truly financially limited. Those in poverty occupy a no-win situation in the contemporary consumer society. They are damned if they consume and damned if they don't and, no matter what they consume, it will be labelled negatively by others who are not experiencing poverty.

A good illustration of how this works in practice can be found through an examination of the term 'chav'. It took on emblematic status in the 1990s as the favoured term to describe those experiencing poverty and became a widely accepted term of abuse towards the British working class, in particular the young working class (Jones, 2011). The term was so widely accepted that, as Jones has pointed out, it was as acceptable at middle-class, supposedly politically enlightened, dinner tables as it was among the country's youth cultures (Nayak, 2000; Shildrick, 2006; McCulloch et al, 2007; Jones, 2011). 'Chav' initially emerged within British youth culture as a term, largely of abuse, by which some young people negatively labelled other groups of young people based primarily on their clothing preferences. Young people's choice of clothing, usually particular brands of sports clothing, came to be closely associated with the 'chav' label, which ultimately became a shorthand and widely known label for anyone experiencing poverty (Nayak, 2000; Shildrick, 2006; McCulloch et al, 2007). What is important about the 'chav' label is how it very quickly entered mainstream vocabulary around class inequality and became a label associated with stigma and disgust.

Other products or consumption practices have been similarly held up and vilified as being vulgar and adding to the widespread demonisation of those in poverty. For example, the widescreen television as it entered the repertoire of everyday consumer behaviour became the overt signifier of poverty shaming for those on low incomes, while retaining its signifier of privilege and status for other groups. As Crossley points out:

> The sofa, the flat-screen televisions and the empty take-away boxes, Styrofoam containers or snacks are all important symbols because they help to locate leisure time and activities of people living in poverty within the home. The political portrayal of the fixity of their physical location neatly symbolises the alleged lumpen nature of their social deprivation and marginalisation. (Crossley, 2017, p 89)

It seems that those in poverty increasingly find themselves between a rock and a hard place in respect of everyday consumption practices. Everyday items such as televisions become markers of inclusion, achievement, wealth and status that is increasingly demanded if people are to 'pass' as non-poor, and are laid before people in an increasing array of seemingly accessible – but for those on the lowest incomes hideously expensive – payment options. Conspicuous consumption can provide a means to avoid the stigmatisation of poverty, but the rules of respectability that govern buying behaviours mean that consumption is never likely to be enough to avoid the stigma and injury of poverty.

Edensor and Millington (2009) have demonstrated how similar 'disgusted' responses occur in relation to the visibly striking festive light displays that have come to be closely associated with supposed working-class excess. Of course, such displays are not confined to those living in poverty or on social housing estates, but once again it is the association between income (or the lack of it) and distaste that is important here. Using an analysis of discussion on social media about Christmas light displays on social housing estates, Edensor and Millington argue that 'excessive forms of house and garden decoration' have the potential to impinge and infringe 'upon the aesthetic convention of "respectable" space' (Edensor and Millington, 2009, p 108), leading to widespread condemnation and abuse on social media sites, where overt displays of this type are maligned for both their supposed tackiness and their cost. The lower social classes or those experiencing poverty become labelled for their supposedly 'crass, excessive and showy consumption' (Edensor and Millington, 2009, p 108). Back agrees in his analysis of festive light displays in Croydon, South London when he argues that 'the festive glow of the decorated working-class homes also reveals the changing relationship between class, culture and the politics of housing' (Back, 2015, p 4) and relates very clearly to 'contemporary class distinctions and histories of class experience' (p 5).

These narratives of negative class labelling and distinction can be challenged by listening more closely to the feelings and experiences of those who are being negatively labelled (Skeggs, 2005; Back, 2015). It was noted above that the popularity of the term 'chav' as a label of class demonisation and stigmatisation was initially associated with youth cultures and, in particular, the wearing of sports clothes by particular groups of young people. Yet research with young people shows how they often purchase particular clothing or products as a means to earn status and worth among their peers. Archer et al (2007) show how, for some young people, their consumption of particular named sportswear provided

> a means for working class young people to generate identity worth or value and to negotiate positions of social

disadvantage and the representational violence that derives from knowing they are 'looked down on' within schools and wider society. (Archer et al, 2007, p 221)

Archer and colleagues have also shown in their research with young people in London who are identified as at risk of dropping out or drifting away from education that sometimes particular items of clothing can help to mitigate the stigma and shame that young people acutely feel (Archer et al, 2010). They reported that young people in their study were 'painfully aware that they were looked down upon by society' (Archer et al, 2010, p 35). Their investment in particular styles of branded clothing could be read as 'attempts to generate capital and to claim value and recognition through alternative means' (p 35). Moreover,

> Identification with and loyalty to particular brands, such as Nike, became a means through which identity was not only performed on the body but etched on the psyche. Brands like Nike were implicated in young people's personal identity constructions, it was a way of 'being me' ...//... this desire to be me, was also heavily policed by peer groups (non-conformity being 'social suicide'). Thus successful performances of style generated currency and status within peer groups and afforded 'safety' from bullying and marginalisation. (Archer et al, 2010, p 36)

Yet the same styles were the source of negative labelling by those in more privileged and powerful positions and could bring young people into conflict, for example, with teachers. The 'Nike style' (wearing trainers and hooded tops) may be positioned by the middle classes as negative, tasteless and signifying danger or threat. This is illustrative of the complex and damaging nature of stigmatisation through consumption practices of those experiencing poverty, whereby consumption can be a source of both value and stigma at the same time. In a similar way Edensor and Millington (2009) have shown how Christmas lights and other similar festive displays in working-class neighbourhoods can have particular sorts of meaning for those engaged in making the displays, despite often being loaded with negative meanings in wider society. Significantly, the interviewees in Edensor and Millington's research stressed their desire to spread joy to others via the displays, and this was particularly the case in respect of close family. Respondents also talked about feeling a sense of community responsibility, as neighbours came to expect the annual displays put on by particular families. The research stresses that the light displayers are not simply victims of 'symbolic violence' but instead attain 'status and a positive sense of identity' (Edensor and Millington, 2009, p 118) in their own locales and social networks. These 'divergent productions proffer contesting ideas about space, community, aesthetics and festivity' and also 'express different contemporary processes of class formation' (p 104). In general, people were either oblivious or dismissive of negative views in respect of their displays. Yet the values of 'celebration, giving and friendliness' (p 113) that dominated the interviewees' accounts are obscured by a discourse of working-class crassness, poor taste and excess.

Kathy Hamilton's research with mothers on low incomes offers a nuanced reading of how the consumption practices of those on low incomes can be better understood. Drawing on in-depth interviews with families living on low incomes, Hamilton argues that 'individuals initiate strategies to avoid the social effects of stigmatisation and alleviate threats to social identity' (Hamilton, 2012, p 74). She argues that young single mothers' investment in buying the 'right' designer brands for their children can be understood in opposing ways. The mothers in her research placed emphasis on conspicuous consumption so as to avoid the social effects of stigmatisation; furthermore, such consumption practices (buying named-brand trainers for children, for example) can 'have a positive impact on the self-esteem of single mothers' (Hamilton, 2012, p 76). Yet, at the same time those very same consumption habits are often demonised and stigmatised by wider society. Hamilton argues that the mothers in her research, while attempting to improve the living standards of their families and provide their children with the accepted trappings of current consumer society, were at the same time feeding into a broader process that fuels further stigmatisation, exclusion and marginalisation. The families were engaged in strategies and behaviours that were an attempt to 'disguise' their poverty (Hamilton, 2012, p 75) and were also understood as an expression of what it meant to be 'being a good mother' (p 83). Similarly, the women in my own research projects were quick to label and castigate other women for their supposed food consumption practices that were often argued to be inappropriate and unhealthy (Shildrick and MacDonald, 2013). In respect of the mothers in Hamilton's research, she concluded that

> Those who follow a strategy of conspicuous consumption to mask poverty encounter the very stigmatisation that they set out to avoid in the first instance. (Hamilton, 2012, p 87)

Research consistently shows that those in poverty often struggle to meet their day-to-day needs and that they work hard to employ strategies to help them do so. Research also shows that families in poverty, and often mothers who have the main responsibility for managing on low incomes, suffer great stress when they are unable to provide their children with the sorts of products that are commonplace among their peers. Birthdays and Christmas are particular pressure points as the pressures to consume and to be seen to consume in the right ways, which confirm respectability and help to disguise the effects of poverty, can be immense (Shildrick et al, 2012a).

Stigma, shame and discrimination

Diane Reay points to the difficulty of separating class practices from class feeling and thinking:

> There is a circularity at play here. It could be argued that it is class thinking and feeling that generates class practices. At the very least there is a generative dynamic between thinking, feeling and practices. ... class thinking and feeling [are] what I term the psychic landscape of social class. (Reay, 2005, p 912)

It is difficult to separate the ways in which stigmatisation and shame work to inform the ways in which poverty is responded to through both policy and everyday practices. We learn more about how poverty propaganda supports particular policy responses to poverty in the next chapter, but some more general issues are raised here. Andrew Sayer has played an instrumental role in highlighting the moral boundaries of social class. In pointing to the moral and immoral sentiments of class he points out that the effects can play out in real and discriminatory ways:

> Class contempt, like other kinds of 'othering' rages from visceral revulsion, disgust and sneering, through the tendency not to see or hear others as people, to the subtlest forms of aversion. In its mildest forms it may merely involve a slight feeling of unease when in the company of others, and may merge into a sense of not belonging rather than hostility towards the other. Even at its mildest class contempt can, on certain occasions, such as job interviews, make a major difference to people's life chances. (Sayer, 2009, p 163)

Experiencing poverty in the UK can mean being subjected to discrimination on the grounds of poverty (Kileen, 2008). This is often manifest in the ways that people feel judged by professionals, as we saw in the section above. Research shows that the stigma and shame of poverty are made worse and often caused by the discriminatory treatment that those experiencing poverty and related disadvantages receive from services aimed at helping them (Hastings, 2009a; 2009b). Research has also shown how those working in organisations working with those in poverty and disadvantaged circumstances can also operate with stereotypical views of their clients' circumstances (Shildrick et al, 2012; Dunn, 2016). In her research on this topic Hastings has shown how

> One manager argued, for example, that the improper disposal of refuse and litter was 'a social thing, people just do it. It's a culture thing: it's not being educated out of them'. Another suggested that 'the people there are just dirty, that's all there is to it'. Front-line operatives often used colourful language to refer to the residents of environmentally problematic neighbourhoods: 'scum', 'lazy people' or, as one street-sweeper claimed: 'there are certain people who are just scruffy bastards'. (Hastings, 2009b, p 219)

Research has also shown that these sorts of stereotypical narratives permeate the experiences of those in poverty. Not only do they translate into discriminatory behaviours being applied to those in disadvantaged circumstances, but they also engender negative feelings of not being treated with respect. Power (2005) has shown how women on 'welfare' in Canada struggled with the ways in which they were treated by people working in the Department of Community Services. She describes how women felt 'humiliated, outraged and bewildered' (Power, 2005, p 647). In particular, they expressed concern about the ways in which what they perceived to be legitimate everyday needs were routinely denied by those in power and the ways in which they were subjected to various forms of surveillance (Power, 2005, p 647). Power also describes the insecurity and fragility of the women's financial situations, which could be determined at any point in time by those with power to allow or prevent them from receiving 'welfare'. Patrick's research has shown the same, whereby those in receipt of 'welfare' are all too aware of how others perceive them, often felt negatively judged by those making decisions about their entitlements and lives (Patrick, 2017).

Research by Fletcher and colleagues has shown how key stakeholders working with claimants operate with 'pervasive, if incorrect, understanding among the UK population of widespread cynical manipulation of the welfare system' (Fletcher et al, 2016, p 176). Respondents in their research used well-worn phrases such as "people do make choices to be on benefits and I do think that should be challenged". One respondent noted that "they're sometimes not very likable characters" (Fletcher et al, 2016, p 176). Stakeholders also recognised that these narratives could be exaggerated, but none the less,

> Stakeholders identified the power of narratives of cynical manipulation in shaping public attitudes to welfare and the presence (albeit exaggerated) of individuals gaming the system and argued that both required a social policy response including conditionality. (Fletcher et al, 2016, p 177)

One of our Teesside interviewees told us about his experiences of being assessed for sickness benefits:

> "They have now got a company, this is a government thing Atos I think it is … they are screening people basically, they're just disallowing everyone's benefit, erm sickness benefit and making them go through the appeal system. Now my problem with that, aw right we know there's too many people claiming sickness benefit who should be seeking Jobseeker's Allowance but my problem with that is, everyone had been treated the same. Basically I feel that we are going the wrong way about it and they are treating people like criminals." (Patrick, aged 49, interviewee in Shildrick et al, 2012b)

A number of challenges around the legality of some 'welfare' reforms have been brought before the courts, and with some success (Leventhal, 2017). The so-called bedroom tax, as it has popularly been dubbed, whereby people are forced to pay for bedrooms that are deemed surplus to their requirements if they live in council or housing association property and claim housing benefit, was ruled illegal for particular cases (Butler, 2016). Yet cases that manage to make it to court are rare. Undertaking a legal challenge is very difficult of course, especially so when people are experiencing poverty and related disadvantages, making them an easy target. ATD Fourth World also points to this class-based discrimination and argues that:

> Discrimination based on the perception of class (sometimes called 'povertyism' in the United Kingdom) constitutes [...] a barrier to people moving out of poverty [... and] perpetuates a lack of knowledge and understanding about the lives of people experiencing poverty. Such attitudes are sometimes based on the view that people living in poverty are inferior or of lesser value. The consequence of povertyism, for those who experience it, is that such attitudes become a driver of a particular policy approach that results in denial of their human rights. (ATD Fourth World, 2016)

The very fact of experiencing poverty means that people are often on the receiving end of things over which they have little or no control. Decisions, actions and, most importantly, power lie in the hands of others. A key factor that drove our cultures of worklessness study (Shildrick et al, 2012b) was the repeated assertion by people working with the unemployed that a key explanation for worklessness was 'generations who have never worked' and that young people growing up in workless families have learned from their parents that to be unemployed is acceptable. It was a genuine puzzlement at the numbers of people working on the ground with the unemployed and who repeated this narrative (as well as its power in everyday political and popular discourse) that drove the study in the first place. Our contacts on the ground were well-informed people, they worked very closely with the workless, so we were puzzled that their views seemed so at odds with our close-up investigations of people's lives gathered over many years in deprived neighbourhoods. Rather than take these assertions at face value as some others have (Mead, 1993; Dunn, 2016), our research took a more critical and in-depth approach to investigating this idea. We undertook in-depth interviews with both practitioners and people experiencing long-term worklessness and dug beneath the surface of opinions and rhetoric to really discover what lay behind these popular ideas.

What was most illuminating in the process of interrogating these ideas with practitioners was how quickly the idea started to crumble away. When practitioners tried to think of particular families that they knew who had never worked, they struggled to think of any. What they more readily drew into their minds were families they knew who had long periods of worklessness in their backgrounds, but rarely were they completely workless. In fact what came to mind were, more accurately, a smaller number of deeply troubled families, often pretty well known to them and who had long periods of worklessness, but usually punctuated by periods of work and who also experienced a whole gamut of other difficulties and problems. These were exactly the sorts of unusual families that we ended up talking to in Teesside and Glasgow (Shildrick et al, 2012b). Negative labelling leads to onerous judgements about how a person should be treated or where the solution to their problems might lie. Povertyism is perhaps the last form of acceptable discrimination in a society that prides itself on equality and acceptance of difference. It allows individual solutions to the problem of unemployment to be given priority with a focus on altering the individual's behaviour in some way, when the root of the problem is far more likely to reside in conditions outside of individuals' control.

Conclusions

Following the seminal work of Skeggs in this field, others have pointed to the progressive and corrosive nature of class conditions for the working classes (Skeggs, 2005). This is not just in terms of decent working opportunities but also in the ways in which the working class are perceived and treated. The mistreatment of those who are in poverty or suffering disadvantage is part of this process. Dorling (2010) suggests that Beveridge's five social evils have been transformed in appearance over recent decades, with idleness being replaced 'by a more general evil of prejudice' (Dorling, 2010, p 6). Throughout this book it has been shown that poverty and working-class life more generally have been subjected to a set of processes that render them problematic in one way or another. In consequence there has been an increase in overt (and covert) prejudice aimed at those experiencing poverty. What is important here is not just the process of making distinctions but also the value – or lack of value – that is attached to particular patterns of consumption or ways of behaving. On the face of it, patterns of consumption may seem to open up opportunities for identity construction, but such developments do not easily transcend social-class differences. As shown above, they often seem to reinforce and support them. Mckenzie points out how the respondents in her study of St Anne's also stayed in St Anne's because 'it provides safety from class prejudice' (Mckenzie, 2015, p xii). Such class prejudice is increasingly reinforced via policy and practice. Mckenzie argues that class prejudice has been institutionalised, particularly through the police, courts and the legal system (Mckenzie, 2015, p xii). Hence, despite the suggestions that there has been a loosening up of class differences, there is much evidence to suggest that social class continues to exert significant influence over people's life chances and life experiences.

SEVEN

Poverty propaganda and reproduction of poverty, power and inequality

Introduction

Writing in 1845, Friedrich Engels argued that

> When an individual inflicts bodily injury upon another, such injury that death results, we call the deed manslaughter; when the assailant knew in advance that injury would be fatal, we call this deed murder. But when society places hundreds of proletarians in such a position that they inevitably meet an early and unnatural death, one which is quite as much a death by violence as that by the sword or the bullet; when it deprives thousands of the necessities of life, places them under conditions in which they cannot live – forces them through the strong arm of the law, to remain in such conditions until death ensues, which is the inevitable consequence – knows that these thousands of victims must perish, yet permits these conditions to remain,its deed is murder just as surely as the deed of the single individual; disguised, malicious murder. (Engels, 1845(2009), p 106)

As the chapters of this book have demonstrated, the most economically marginalised in our society, including those experiencing sometimes very deep poverty, are facing deliberately sustained, brutal and unforgiving assaults on their life chances and conditions. The quotation above is no less relevant today than it was when it was written well over 150 years ago. Indeed we could argue that it is even more relevant, given the wealth and general increases in living standards that have ensued since. Those on lower incomes have long faced poorer health and life chances in general but since 2010 austerity has added an additional, unnecessary and particularly brutal layer of disadvantage to already difficult life conditions. The increased incidence of early death (Dorling, 2017), along with starvation and the rise in forced destitution, might sound like they belong in a different century, but they are the new reality for many in a callous and unforgiving economic system that creates hostile, life-limiting and in some cases life-destroying conditions for those on low incomes. This chapter looks at the consequences of poverty propaganda in terms of policy responses to poverty that make life worse for those on low incomes. It also explores how and why these policy developments are tolerated – and even desired – by a general public that largely tends to buy into the value of poverty propaganda at least on some level. The chapter looks into the wider impacts of poverty propaganda and asks who benefits from its production. It is argued that the production of poverty propaganda is a deliberate product of neoliberal capitalist regimes, like in the UK, whereby inequality is entrenched and deepened to benefit capitalist winners, further penalising and marginalising its losers. What should now be clear to readers is that poverty propaganda – *ideas* about poverty – produces real effects and influence on the way that those experiencing poverty are treated, on how poverty as a condition is responded to and, ultimately, on how those experiencing poverty feel about their own lives. Throughout this book we have seen that much of the political and popular debate around poverty owes more to a set of powerful ideas that work together to produce a generic narrative around poverty than to any sensible or well-informed debate about the realities of poverty in 21st-century Britain. This poverty propaganda takes different forms that allow it to work effectively across policy, political and public landscapes. It works to misshape understandings about poverty and to stigmatise those who experience the condition and allows for punitive policy responses that serve to worsen the condition and the positions of those who experience it. In this chapter three key issues will be discussed. Firstly, the chapter looks at how poverty propaganda works to allow punitive and discriminatory policies to be enacted towards those experiencing poverty and related disadvantages. Secondly, it examines the ways in which public opinion reacts to poverty propaganda and how this helps to support its effects and its power. Crucially, poverty propaganda works to divide the working class, creating divisions between populations who have more in common than they tend to readily accept. Finally, the chapter looks at how all of these factors contribute to a deepening inequality that has real and direct benefits for groups that are economically advantaged.

Inequality, poverty propaganda and policies that hurt the most disadvantaged

The march of neoliberal capitalism in countries such as the UK has meant that the state has been rolled back as risks and responsibilities have been shifted very firmly onto individuals. The pursuit of profits and the prioritisation of a free market have worked to entrench inequalities to the point that the UK is now one of the most unequal countries in the world (Piketty, 2014). For those on the lowest incomes this is not good news. Those on lower incomes fare particularly badly in an economic system that has long afforded advantages to the better-off. Additionally, the power to conform to the increasingly manufactured and widely promoted expectations of inclusion, particularly via overt consumption practices, also works to hide the limits that poverty places on life choices. Families and individuals are compelled either to do their utmost to adhere to the accepted norms of inclusion (by, for example, hiding or trying to mitigate their poverty as we saw in Chapter Three) or to risk being labelled as failures, and culpable for their situations.

As we saw in Chapter Two, increasingly people, particularly those reliant on out-of-work benefits, have been deliberately cast as problematic. The notion that those claiming out-of-work benefits are lazy and undeserving has been deliberately orchestrated to undermine support for out-of-work benefits and has managed to do so with a good deal of success (British Social Attitudes, 2017). The notion of 'welfare' dependency, as a negative state rather than simply a neutral state, has been a powerful and deliberately deployed device that has increasingly infected policy documents and public and political debate around disadvantage. The deliberately harsh tones used across these forums and that emphasise problematic drug and alcohol use or variously and multiply 'troubled families' are used to evoke anger at the 'welfare' state, which is generally held responsible for supporting individually problematic behaviours and hence unworthy lives and lifestyles.

In Chapter Two we learned about poverty propaganda and discussed a number of examples. This chapter is more concerned with the crafting of poverty propaganda as well as the consequences and purpose of it. Here we concentrate on the crafting of poverty propaganda through policy documents, political discourse and via the media. These three key sites of power and influence constitute the core of the poverty propaganda machine. Policy documents that go a long way to informing actual policy and the tone and nature of popular and political discussions on poverty have increasingly shifted their focus and language to include more negative and pejorative terms in reference to 'welfare'. This process has been in train for some time, but Wiggan has shown that the language of policy documents has become more firmly wedded to notions of 'welfare' dependency since the election of the Coalition government in 2010 (Wiggan, 2012). He argues, and his analysis of policy documents shows very clearly, how the more supportive approach to conditionality that characterised New Labour virtually disappeared under the Coalition, which moved to very clearly 'construct the persistence of poverty and unemployment as originating in the poor choices and behaviours of individuals' (Wiggan, 2012, p 400). Thus,

> It would be churlish to fail to acknowledge that threaded through the Coalition's 2010 Green Paper, *21st Century welfare* and White Paper, *Universal Credit: welfare that works* is a commendable acknowledgment of the financial constraints and barriers low income families experience when transitioning into the labour market. Yet the terms that dominate – worklessness and dependency – construct the persistence of poverty and unemployment as originating in the poor choices and behaviour of individuals. An expensive, well-meaning system of state support is portrayed as not only ineffective but as reinforcing social problems by permitting people to make the 'wrong' choices due to poor incentives in the benefit system, with devastating consequences for poor families. (Wiggan, 2012, p 400)

We also need to consider who is shaping debates and policy and ask why it is better for those in power to present these unusual and rare cases of deeply troubled individuals or families as representative of people claiming out-of-work benefits and to focus on supposed personal difficulties rather than, for example, to spend as much time bemoaning the lack of decent jobs. Tom Slater (2012) provides a powerful argument for the 'wilful *institutional ignorance*' (p 3) surrounding 'welfare' reform, using the word 'agnotology', a term first used by Robert Proctor to describe 'the study of ignorance making'. Slater argues that 'concepts have been strategically developed by a conservative think tank (the *Centre for Social Justice*) to manufacture doubt with respect to the structural causes of unemployment and poverty' (Slater, 2012, p 3). We saw in Chapter Two how the trope of 'social justice' became a mantra for the infliction of social injustice. Bob Holman, who died in 2016, was a well-respected poverty campaigner (and later academic) wrote insightfully from the ground about the realities of poverty. He worked with Duncan Smith for a time, convinced (or more likely, I suspect, desperately willing to hope) that the latter was intending to do good work while in government that might do something towards addressing the root causes of poverty (which Holman was all too familiar with). Yet, by 2012, amid the swingeing cuts to 'welfare' orchestrated by Duncan Smith in his time as Work and Pensions Secretary (2010–16), many, including Holman, had turned their backs on Duncan Smith and the government he represented. In 2012 Holman concluded that, under pressure to make huge budget cuts and to cover his own failures, Duncan Smith had shifted his perspective back to 'blaming those experiencing poverty for their own predicament, citing poor parenting, drug and alcohol addiction, laziness and the break up of families' (Holman, 2012). As Holman himself concluded, 'he [Duncan Smith] wept at the plight of the poor (in his widely reported initial visit to Easterhouse in Scotland in 2002), yet now hands out punishments that must bring tears to their eyes' (Holman, 2012). Yet, the Centre for Social Justice has been hugely influential in both directing government policy towards poverty and disseminating its key messages to a wider audience (often being given key media slots on main-channel news reports). Slater concludes that:

> Viewed through an agnotological lens, the CSJ [Centre for Social Justice] publications recast the public debate on poverty, welfare and unemployment in three ways. Firstly they divert public attention away from the structural and institutional failures that lie behind poverty, and from the nature and extent of inequality in Britain. Second, they exploit public doubt ('not knowing') with respect to the causal agents of poverty and inequality, in an attempt to make the uncertain certain, and to reduce and simplify a complex history of political economic shifts into a series of easily digestible behavioural catchphrases. Third, they ignore any alternative approaches to the problem of poverty (and welfare) in Britain. (Slater, 2012, p 14)

Importantly, they also pave the way for punitive policies to be accepted or tolerated rather than challenged. Politicians rarely consult academic research, especially that which challenges their courses of action or calls into question their approaches to poverty. As Slater observes,

> Politicians rarely consult published social science research
> unless it supports the policies they want to pursue (witness,
> for instance, the fact that *not a single social scientist* was a
> member of any of the CSJ working groups studying the five
> 'pathways to poverty'). Instead they depend on neat sound
> bites drawn from surveys that measure nothing more than
> the worldview of the think tank that commissions them.
> (Slater, 2012, p 8)

What is important to highlight here is the power of the Centre for Social Justice, not just in influencing and contributing to Conservative policy development and practice but in getting its ideas out to the general public. Repeated invitations to present their work on popular mainstream television, for example news programmes or others like the BBC's *Newsnight*, enable the core messages to reach a generic audience. This is a privilege that is much less often offered to academic researchers and has important implications for the power and influence of poverty propaganda. Playing up themes of personal responsibility not only detracts attention from the structural drivers of poverty (and particular governments' roles in either alleviating or spreading the condition) but also allows policies that punish people to be brought forward with little complaint. This has been especially apparent since the election of the Coalition government led by the Conservatives in 2010, whose cuts in the name of austerity have been pursued with vigour. As Levitas has pointed out in respect of austerity measures, 'the driving imperative of this policy is to force down public sector spending. Cuts in welfare spending impinge directly on the poor, the young, the sick and the disabled' (Levitas, 2013, p 323). Austerity has been largely presented as being in the interests of the country as a whole. The previous Prime Minister, David Cameron, liked to remind people that it was his belief that it was 'fair that those with broad shoulders should bear the greater load' (Cameron, 2010). This rhetoric does a lot of powerful work and helps to hide the realities of where the axes fall:

> It is increasingly the more disadvantaged households,
> particularly those with dependent children, who are feeling
> the greatest effects of austerity and retrenchment in welfare
> benefits and public services and are seeing the biggest impact
> in their everyday lives. (Kennett et al, 2015, p 640)

Poverty in Britain is not the result of the economic crash, as we have seen through the pages of this book, but recent policy developments have served to deepen and extend the condition. In particular, austerity measures and cuts made in the name of austerity place more punitive and onerous demands on those experiencing poverty. This is not only a strategy that inflicts further individual harm and hardship on families and individuals but one that will worsen levels of inequality between those at the top and those the bottom of the economic (and social class) structure (Savage, 2015) in a country that is already one of the most unequal in the world.

Atkinson et al (2012) argue that the results of austerity and the recession have produced a 'stratified impact' across numerous areas of social life, including family life, consumption and education, but the effects have been particularly damaging for those on limited incomes. Cuts to public services can have disastrous impacts for those on low incomes, who tend to be more reliant on them (and who generally lack the resources to replace them with private services). The pace and scale of cuts has certainly been challenging for local authorities, which have suffered some of the biggest cuts overall – although these have been very uneven, with the most severe cuts being imposed in some of the most deprived local authorities. In part, this was due to the withdrawal of funding that had been given under New Labour, which had been keen to support disadvantaged communities and made significant strides towards increasing incomes for those experiencing poverty. New Labour's approach, particularly around subsidising low wages through tax credits, had its limitations but the commitment to ending child poverty that was made under Tony Blair (and now often forgotten under harsher attitudes towards poverty and Tony Blair's own fall from political grace) was historically ground breaking. While the targets were not likely to be fully realised by 2020, by the time Labour lost power in 2010 great strides had been made (Hirsch, 2008). Of course, these positives have been reversed, and worse, since 2010, but it is worth recalling this, if only to remind ourselves that things can – where there is the will – be done differently.

People on lower incomes have been badly impacted by cuts, and by 'welfare' reforms more specifically and, in particular, changes to out-of-work benefits. Many families have been hit by a 'perfect storm' of changes and cuts to their incomes. Services have been cut since 2011. Hastings and colleagues' use of the concepts of 'early' and 'later' austerity is useful here (Hastings et al, 2015, p 617). They identify the period 2011–13 as 'early austerity', when the councils were making 'back office' cuts, mostly via efficiency savings, often shedding 'back office' rather than 'front line' posts and making other, less visible savings. However, as Hastings et al point out, there is a limit to these sorts of savings, which are likely to have been exhausted in the early phase of austerity. It is in the 'later' phase, which they identify as 2013–16, that front-line cuts are more likely to bite (Hastings et al, 2015, p 617). At the time of writing many services, including social care and social services, were reporting that they were in crisis and had been cut to the bone. The notion that 'welfare' and, particularly, out-of-work benefits, are a deserved and necessary target for cuts has been supported by a steady stream of poverty propaganda, whose effects serve to bolster the confidence of a government that is determined to push ahead with stringent cuts to the livelihoods of those people with the least. An acceptance that at least a proportion of the workless are work-shy has meant that conditionality has become not just palatable but necessary, and harsh conditionality is now at the heart of the 'welfare' system (Dwyer and Wright, 2014; Wright, 2012; 2014; 2015).

In many respects the poverty propaganda that we have read about in this book has paved the way for punitive austerity measures to be tolerated and largely accepted. This must, to a large degree, explain the absence of public anger despite the widespread publicity given to high-profile cases of austerity suicides and people who have died as a result of austerity measures (Dorling et al 2017).

Stanley (2015) notes that the issue of austerity is actually a 'battle over ideas'. Gamble (2014) has similarly drawn on the idea of 'statecraft' to illustrate how particular sound bites and lines of argument were drawn upon beyond the 2010 general election to foster a particular narrative around deficit reduction and the necessity of austerity. In doing so, the Coalition government changed the terms of the debate and created 'a new dividing line with Labour on the wrong side of it, as the party who had got the country into the mess in the first place' (Gamble, 2014, p 6). Under this new 'rhetoric of hard times' (Gamble, 2014, p 1) the public have been largely convinced that austerity is necessary (Stanley, 2015), but, as Reay argues, 'austerity is primarily for those who already have the least while the secure upper echelons of the middle class and our political and economic elites remain largely untouched' (Reay, 2012, p 33). Simon Pemberton's work is useful here when he develops the concepts of 'social harm' and 'harmful societies' (Pemberton, 2016). Commenting on austerity, he argues that full analysis of the harms done by these policy measures will become apparent only in the fullness of time:

> If we want to articulate the devastating scale and extent
> of the damage that has been inflicted we need to produce
> accounts that document the full range of injustices that

austerity has inflicted. Social harm analysis must begin to piece together this evidence. As sufficient time series data emerges it will become easier to do this; nevertheless prima facie the emerging analysis is already damning. (Pemberton, 2016, p 155)

At the moment in the UK the realities of poverty and the ways in which the most vulnerable members of our society are being treated have been largely obscured by a wave of propaganda. As we can see from the brief discussion here, austerity measures play to a neoliberal narrative that supports the escalation of gross inequalities of life chances and life experiences and dictates poverty as an individual failing. As Pring (2017) argues in respect of disabled people, they have had to resort to the criminal justice system and the United Nations to try to uphold their human rights. The government has not simply chosen to plough on with harmful reforms, regardless of the human costs; it has deliberately tried to deflect attention from the numerous cases of sometimes simply horrific accounts of workfare or the brutality of experiences of disabled people who are reliant on 'welfare'. It has drowned these real-life horror stories, quite literally submerging them under a relentless deluge of stories about supposed 'welfare scroungers'. An EU report examining violations of the European Social Charter has pointed to violations in the UK in respect of rates of benefits that, the report argues, are 'manifestly inadequate' (EU, 2016) and fall below 40% of the Eurostat median equivalised income. In a small but telling example of how poverty propaganda works, the then Minister for Work and Pensions, Iain Duncan Smith, quickly dismissed the notion that any more could possibly be spent on 'welfare':

It is lunacy for the Council of Europe to suggest welfare payments need to increase when we paid out £204 billion in benefits and pensions last year. (Duncan Smith, 2014)

It is indeed telling that most of the 'welfare' bill is given over to pensions, yet discussion of this 'welfare' benefit rarely, if ever, attracts the levels of poisonous debate that out-of-work benefits do. A search of the *Daily Mail*, one of the main media outlets that has continually supported the dissemination of poverty propaganda, around this particular story revealed only one main article (despite many about the supposed illegal status of many 'benefit' claimants), which was framed wholly in terms of the UN causing 'outrage' by launching an investigation into the UK 'welfare' system (Doyle, 2014). This particular story focuses mostly on a number of Conservative MPs, including Duncan Smith quoted above, and is framed to belittle the importance of what the UN is saying and to assert Britain's (and the UK's) right to deal with its own domestic policies in the way it wants. The article is pejorative about ministers from other countries, referring to the Brazilian housing 'rapporteur' as a 'former Marxist dubbed the "Brazil Nut"' (Doyle, 2014) and citing one Conservative as referring to the influence of the 'looney left' (Doyle, 2014). Here we can very clearly see not only how poverty propaganda is constructed to deliver a particular message that presents the welfare state in particular and misleading ways but how those messages are repeated and reinforced by powerful media such as the *Daily Mail* and the senior and powerful political figures whose words are given space in the day-to-day reporting of political life. ATD Fourth World argues that

> Impoverished individuals and communities face targeted persecution and exploitation from more powerful members of society. This often occurs with the complicity of the state, in both developed and developing countries. Throughout history, people living in extreme poverty have been deported, institutionalized, incarcerated, forcibly removed from their families, sterilized and, in times of dearth, left to starve. (ATD Fourth World, 2013, p 7)

In a wealthy country such as ours removing meagre and insufficient 'welfare' payments from people who are vulnerable, via benefit sanctions, is not just cruel: it is obscene. Forcing people who very often are facing a range of difficulties and vulnerabilities to somehow try to survive on fresh air is not only nonsensical and counterproductive but archaic. State-inflicted destitution, no matter what the supposed misdemeanour, has no place in a democratic, wealthy nation and has consequences for us all, not just those who feel the full force of the sanctions. The United Nations has expressed concern about this, as we noted in Chapter Three.

> The UN Committee on Economic, Social and Cultural Rights has expressed 'serious concern' about the impact of what it calls 'regressive policies on the enjoyment of economic and social rights' in a damning report on the UK. Over a period of months, the UN committee spoke with government officials, the UK human rights commissions and civil society groups. And now it concludes that austerity

measures and social security reform breach the UK's international human rights obligations. (United Nations Human Rights, 2016)

Of course, human rights are not particularly high up on the current government's list of priorities, other than in respect of its plans to repeal the Human Rights Act (Stone, 2016). With regard to the shaming of people experiencing poverty, Walker has argued that 'shaming is wrong, and probably illegal' (Walker, 2014, p 194). Walker asserts that the 2013 resolution of the UN General Assembly on extreme poverty (based on numerous pieces of international human rights legislation) is very clear in its statement on this issue: 'Extreme poverty and exclusion from society constitute a violation of human dignity and ... urgent national and international action is therefore required to eliminate them' (cited in Walker, 2014, p 195).

The following sub-section looks at the impact of poverty propaganda on public opinion and shows how it works to mitigate potential dissent about the ways in which people experiencing poverty are treated.

Poverty propaganda and public opinion

In order for particular behaviours to be accepted and endorsed, the general public need to be convinced of their efficacy. Most politicians are very mindful of public opinion, as in the end it is public opinion that determines whether or not MPs have jobs and whether or not particular parties can gain – and keep – political power. People's opinions on poverty are important, hence the critical work done by those currently in power, to ensure that poverty propaganda works effectively. Pykett (2014) argues that 'after a sustained period of denigrating and responsibilizing the poor, arguably heightening over the last two decades, it is perhaps no surprise that the attitudes of the mainstream media, the right-wing press, the Conservative-led coalition government, and the "general public" seem to have largely converged'. It is difficult to be completely precise about attitudes towards poverty, as they are often submerged within attitudes towards slightly differing things. Most research has tended to look at attitudes towards 'welfare' or the welfare state. Here there is consensus about a general hardening of attitudes (Deeming, 2015; Geiger-Baumberg and Meueleman, 2016; British Social Attitudes, 2017). This is something that also strongly impacts upon those claiming 'welfare', as we saw in Chapter Six. Hudson and colleagues caution against reading too much change into public attitudes and posit that, in fact, evidence would suggest that there has always been a fair amount of negativity towards the welfare state and those who claim out-of-work benefits (Hudson et al, 2016). It might also be the case that there is more 'ambivalence' in people's attitudes than is commonly assumed, as Geiger-Baumberg and Meueleman argue (2016, p 304). The British Social Attitudes Survey looked at attitudes towards 'welfare' and found that there was strong support for reducing spending on 'welfare' for the unemployed and couples without children and for more limits on when benefits can be accessed (British Social Attitudes Survey data, 2017). Irwin has looked more broadly at attitudes towards inequality; again, she too finds more room for nuance in people's attitudes when we think about inequality more broadly (Irwin, 2016). She argues that her data

> Echoes extant evidence showing that inequality matters to people, who are critical and concerned about its extent. Many commented negatively on the growing divide between 'haves' and 'have-nots'. High earners perceived the growth of an under-class and the diminution of opportunities, while low-income participants were more likely to emphasise injustice and struggle. (Irwin, 2016, p 14)

There is also much evidence that the general public care about fairness and lack of opportunity (Irwin, 2016). They also generally want to believe in the idea of meritocracy, which, as we saw in Chapter Five, in part helps to hide the realities of class advantage and disadvantage. Many of the media programmes that have proliferated over recent years and that claim to depict the lives of those experiencing poverty and related disadvantages – such as *Benefits Street* – clearly work to manipulate and present a caricature of poverty and work effectively to produce poverty propaganda. However, it is important to recognise that the messages they produce, no matter how cleverly crafted, are not simply absorbed without critique. In Series Two of *Benefits Street* (filmed in Teesside, interestingly enough) we meet Julie, a woman who had worked until she was forced to give up work to care for her severely disabled son. The fact that Julie had been working was cleverly and deliberately not revealed until further into the programme, in order not to disrupt the 'welfare dependency' narratives that dominate the programme. When Julie's son, Reagan, died suddenly in the final programme there was an outpouring of sympathy for her on social media. There is more work to be done on how more positive or sympathetic framing of social problems can be tapped into so as to more accurately and positively shape opinions on poverty.

In a not dissimilar way the award-winning BBC documentary *Poor Kids* that was aired on television in 2012 also met with a somewhat mixed response. The programme provided an interesting example of a graphic and powerful style of filmmaking that realistically portrayed the impacts of poverty (in a not dissimilar way to the film *I, Daniel Blake* in 2016). Unusually, the documentary told the stories of Courtney (aged 8), from Bradford, Paige (10), from Glasgow and brother and sister Sam (11) and Kayleigh (16), from Leicester, all of whom were experiencing deep childhood poverty. Their life stories were very different, but the experiences of deep poverty were ones that the children shared. The programme is filmed wholly from the point of view of the children and told in their words. Despite not being shown at peak viewing times, the programme was watched by 2.5 million viewers when it aired and another 1 million on BBC iPlayer. It trended worldwide on Twitter after it was aired and the BBC TV blog page received the most comments ever attributed to a programme. Social media comments about programmes on poverty tend to vary between those that are reasonably sympathetic to the plight of people in poverty and others that are much more negative. The negative commentary can be particularly vitriolic and plays to the personal blaming and stereotyping of those in poverty. Bunker et al's analysis of the audiences watching these sorts of programmes showed that, while opinions were generally split between those who viewed poverty more sympathetically after watching and those whose negative views hardened, the vast majority of people still cited drug and alcohol problems as a key driver of poverty. Seventy-eight per cent reported this as an important factor in explaining poverty, making it the most popular response (Bunker et al, 2015) Bunker et al (2015) have shown that, in general, 'documentary'-style, real-life, fly-on-the-wall documentaries about poverty are popular with the general public and attract higher-than-average viewing figures. The ways in which people relate to and understand these programmes often owe a significant amount to poverty propaganda and their own propensity to distance themselves from the condition and its popular portrayals. The comments on the *Poor Kids* documentary were similarly varied. Many people contacted the BBC to see how they could directly assist the children in the programme by buying them clothing or items for their homes. Many felt sympathy for the children who were the focus of the programme, but then moved on to blame the supposed behaviours of the parents for their predicament, playing to the general and widespread discourse of irresponsibility among those experiencing poverty. Others sought to share their own experiences of poverty, generally emphasising their own ability to manage poverty, thus setting themselves apart from the people in the documentary. For example, one commenter on the BBC blog claimed that

> I am poor, a single parent on a large council estate in London. I work full-time and do everything I can to give my child a good upbringing. We never go hungry. We do a wealth of entertaining and interesting things for free. I save and manage a weeks camping holiday a year. (BBC TV blog comment, 7 June 2011)

While it is clear that there is complexity and inconsistency in people's views around various dimensions of inequality in contemporary Britain, the area in which perhaps there is the most convergence is the belief in poverty propaganda. The idea that at least a proportion of those experiencing poverty and related disadvantages are responsible for their own predicament is extremely widespread (Irwin, 2016). There may be differences in beliefs about the volume of supposed 'welfare scroungers', but most people tend to accept that at least on some level there are people who are undeserving of state support. In addition, most people are keen to distance themselves from the stigma and shame of poverty and this produces a situation whereby even those experiencing deep poverty and widespread disadvantages are keen to disassociate from the condition (Shildrick and MacDonald, 2013). Asking people about poverty and whether it was something that affected their lives was a difficult but revealing conversation in our interviews. Predictably, few people believe that real poverty exists in Britain. As outlined elsewhere in this book, rising general standards of living have done much to mask poverty. Interviewees were also keen to disassociate from the condition of poverty and the negative, victim-blaming discourses that are so associated with it (Shildrick and MacDonald, 2013). Other researchers, such as Garthwaite (2016a; 2016b) and Patrick (2016; 2017), have encountered the same tendencies among their research participants.

Interestingly, in our projects, while interviewees were keen to disassociate from poverty they also were often quick to apply the labels of 'scrounger' to others (Shildrick and MacDonald, 2013). Such is the power and reach of poverty propaganda that even those living in deprived neighbourhoods suspect their neighbours of being 'welfare' cheats and it is this power to seduce people from all social and economic backgrounds that make poverty propaganda so effective. It also produces one of its most divisive and destructive elements. Dividing the working class may be politically advantageous to those who have more economic and other resources (see Shildrick, 2018, forthcoming) but it does little for the working class themselves. Recently the Runnymede Trust, in collaboration with the Centre for Labour and Social Studies (CLASS), called for the 'building of shared interests among the multi-racial working class' (Runnymede and CLASS, 2017, p 3). This is a crucially valuable and important point. Elsewhere in the book have I written about the messy middle, where people generally tend to self-locate (if they think about it at all). A divided working class is, of course, less politically powerful than it would be otherwise. When the current Prime Minister, Theresa May, appeals to 'those who are just about managing' she is using a cleverly crafted rhetorical device that, as she is no doubt well aware, will appeal across most socioeconomic statuses, from the 'squeezed middle' who have seen their incomes fall to those in deep poverty and reliant on out-of-work benefits, who also tend to dissociate from the poorest and believe themselves to be 'managing' (Shildrick and MacDonald, 2013). Poverty propaganda helps to reproduce a class system that keeps those in poverty in place and, at the same time, reproduces intergenerational wealth and power. The following sub-section explores this issue further and asks directly what benefits poverty propaganda accrues, and for whom.

Power, profits and the reproduction of inequality

Poverty propaganda has harmful effects and leads to punitive and harmful policies that impact on those experiencing poverty. Austerity measures have been enacted that harm those on the lowest incomes and further entrench inequalities. For Cooper and Whyte, the key purpose of austerity is to further cement growing inequalities of wealth and opportunity and protect 'concentrations of elite wealth and power' (Cooper and Whyte, 2017, p 11). As with any form of action where there are losers, there are also winners. Tyler's work has been instrumental and very powerful in documenting 'neoliberal Britain from the bottom up, ... the abject forms of inequality and injustice which neoliberalism effects and the resistance and revolt to which it gives rise' (Tyler, 2013, p 3). In a broader thesis of the effects of neoliberalism on different groups, Tyler offers

> A *thick* social and cultural account of neoliberalism as a form of governance – concentrating in particular on the mechanisms through which public consent is procured

for policies and practices that affect inequalities and fundamentally corrode democracy. (Tyler, 2013, p 5)

Hence, in Tyler's view, 'stigmatisation operates as a form of governance which legitimises the reproduction and entrenchment of inequalities and injustices which impact upon us all' (Tyler, 2013, p 212). Key to this is the perpetuation of the notion that life conditions are deserved and that this applies as much to those experiencing poverty as to those who do not. There are many economic and capital interests that are strongly invested in the success of poverty propaganda. Welfare-to-work agencies have proved to be big financial winners in the process of 'welfare' reform, and some of their financial dealings have not been without controversy. Since the days of New Labour it has been common practice to pay contractors on the basis of their record in helping people into work, the payments often being graded by the supposed 'difficulty' of particular client groups. In respect of the current Work Programme:

> Claimants referred to the Work Programme were to be assigned to contractors, whose job was to help them into work by providing help with CVs, job applications and with more substantial barriers such as drug and alcohol problems. These contractors were paid on the basis of their record in moving claimants into work and keeping them there. Although it replaced Labour's Flexible New Deal, the Work Programme continued Labour 's approach of giving contractors from the private and voluntary sectors the freedom to operate, guided only by the understanding that they would be paid solely on the basis of their results. (Field and Forsey, 2016, p 16)

The focus on out-of-work benefit claimants and the suggestion that they are in some way flawed or responsible for their plight detracts not only from a discussion about what causes unemployment, and in particular the role that the labour market might play, but also from questions of who might benefit from efforts directed to the problem. Similarly, in respect of the Housing Benefit cap introduced in 2013, much was made of families receiving significant sums of money to live in particular properties, asserting the unfairness of people on out-of-work benefits living in properties that could not be afforded by people on average wages. Yet, Housing Benefit payments are essentially a financial transaction between a landlord and the state, so the idea that

EIGHT

Conclusions[1]

Alcock (2006, p 200) notes that

> To identify oneself as poor is to identify oneself as having a problem and being in need of help. This is a negative categorisation, which people desperately trying to survive, perhaps with dignity, in a hostile world may not willingly and openly wish to adopt.

It is the core contention of this book that the nature of poverty and the ways in which it is understood and conceptualised both politically and popularly have changed since the mid-1970s, with the pace and nature of change accelerating since 2010. Many myths and untruths abound and the realities of poverty and the limitations it places on people's lives and life chances have been obscured behind a divisive and deliberately generic set of discussions and sound bites that play up ideas of 'welfare dependency' and troubled individuals and families. The realties and hardships of poverty have been masked and lost behind myths and untruths, while poverty as a condition affects more and more British citizens. Such is the power of poverty propaganda that even those people who are badly affected by poverty and its effects are keen to disassociate themselves from the condition (Shildrick and MacDonald, 2013). Deliberately punitive policies that deepen poverty and extend the condition to more people have become acceptable to a general public that is largely seduced by the simple notion that those experiencing poverty are culpable for their own situations. Failure to escape poverty is thus both an individual failing and a source of pain and shame (Walker and Chase, 2014). The lack of decent work opportunities, the growth of insecure and low-paid employment and its role in fostering poverty manage to go largely unremarked upon. Further, the brutal and humiliating treatment of many forced to rely on out-of-work benefits is also allowed to pass with barely a murmur (Cooper and Whyte, 2017). The growth of what I term the messy middle and the desire of most people to belong somewhere within it and to disassociate themselves from poverty and related disadvantages means that poverty can continue to be at one and the same time both normalised and also stigmatised and misrepresented. What, then, can we conclude from the various chapters of this book? Its overriding arguments are as follows.

- In the current economic and political context the realities of poverty as a condition are obscured from view by the increasing preponderance of poverty propaganda that breeds myths and untruths about poverty and those who experience the condition.
- The main causes of poverty in Britain are inadequate and poor-quality employment opportunities and an increasingly insufficient 'welfare' system that fails to provide social security for people when they require it.
- The experience of poverty is deeply debilitating and damaging; it is a condition of limit that works to reproduce class inequality and disadvantage.
- Poverty propaganda facilities punitive and cruel policies towards poverty (for example, the current austerity and 'welfare' reform agendas) and helps such policies to masquerade as necessary, just and fair.
- The success of poverty propaganda means that even those experiencing deep poverty are keen to dissociate themselves from poverty.
- Poverty is deeply damaging, not only for those who experience the condition, but also for society more widely, but at the same time, it does provide economic benefits for some.

Poverty: exploring the myths

This book set out to explore some of the myths that exist in Britain around poverty and its causes and consequences. Several key untruths about poverty, defined here as poverty propaganda, have been discussed across the pages of the book. These untruths take various forms and virtually saturate popular and political conversations about poverty and related disadvantages. As a consequence of poverty propaganda the realities of poverty and what causes it are almost completely obscured from view. Poverty propaganda comes in some quite diverse forms, ranging from the notion that people are fraudulently claiming out-of-work benefits to the idea that generic segments of the population are problematic in terms of their morals, behaviours and values. The success of poverty propaganda comes in part from its unwieldy nature that allows it to stigmatise multiple, diffuse and very loosely defined populations, ranging from people experiencing poverty to claimants of out-of-work benefits to social housing tenants, among any number of others. Further, it is this blanket stigmatisation that allows poverty propaganda to wield so much power, as even those experiencing deep poverty and related disadvantages do all they can to distance themselves from its tarnished and stigmatised reputation. In some respects the increasing importance of consumption and the desire to avoid the stigma and shame of poverty force people to try to mask or mitigate these limitations. This is particularly marked for parents who work tirelessly to try to ensure that their children are not deprived of things that other children take for granted. For Nunn and Tepe-Belfrage it is the ability to consume in particular ways and make particular choices that increasingly marks out the included from the excluded, with those unable to rise to the demands of inclusion (or to present themselves as doing so) 'increasingly ghettoised conceptually and politically' (Nunn and Tepe-Belfrage, 2017, p 120).

'Welfare' occupies a central place in poverty propaganda in Britain. In neoliberal societies such as Britain risks are shifted away from the state and onto individuals and families (Hall and Lamont, 2013). The welfare state in its broader sense played a fundamental role in affording benefits to the working classes in the post-war period, but since the 1970s these benefits have been continually eroded. Poverty propaganda helps to make these shifts in responsibility more palatable and less troublesome to the general public than they might otherwise be. Successive governments have played up the notion of supposed 'welfare' dependency as a means of garnering support for punitive policies that undermine and roll back the role of the state in supporting families and individuals (Hall and Lamont, 2013). This trend has been particularly marked since 2010 but the idea that some populations in society are somehow adrift from the rest has been a recurrent theme in political debates since the 1980s. The language has changed over time but there has been a marked shift in tone since 2010, to place narratives of troubled and troubling populations at the centre of popular and political discussions about poverty and related disadvantages.

The focus on troubled behaviours (such as criminality or problematic drug or alcohol use) and general individual pathologies has become ubiquitous in British political and popular discourse, to the point that insidious stereotypes dominate public, popular and political discussion. For those forced to rely on out-of-work benefits, it is simply untrue to suggest that life is not financially limited. Out-of-work benefits keep people in poverty, sometimes very deep poverty, and increasingly, in all too many instances, force people into destitution (Fitzpatrick et al, 2016). Out-of-work benefits do not afford anything other than an extremely limited form of income, as we have seen across the pages of this book, and increasingly people have to jump through more and more hoops to get any income at all. The notion that people can live well if, for example, they are reliant on out-of-work benefits is supported by and further feeds into the idea that people on out-of-work benefits are work-shy, that they are content to remain out of work.

The idea that people prefer to stay on out-of-work benefits rather than take work is often repeated. It takes the form of references to 'welfare dependency' in policy documents and is reinforced via political messages that stress the importance of getting people into work. Indeed it is this one message that has dominated much of the recent debate around the welfare state. The popular caricature of the workers and the shirkers plays a powerful role in cementing the idea that some people are undeserving. Given that all the evidence shows that even those in deeply disadvantaged circumstances quite correctly reject the shirker label, this form of poverty propaganda becomes a very powerful political tool.

The frequent assertion in popular and political narratives that people on out-of-work benefits are claiming something not only that the 'hard workers' don't get but that they might not even be entitled to is also a theme that dominates in poverty propaganda. People can be labelled as getting something they don't deserve for any number of reasons (from the idea that they are lazy and work-shy, or because they are claiming out-of-work benefits that they are not entitled to, for example, by claiming to be sick when in fact they are perfectly capable of working). That 'welfare' claimants are cheating the system is a common refrain and often repeated by various forms of poverty propaganda. It is something that resonates with the general public, as most report that there is a significant amount of undeserved or unnecessary claiming (Baumberg Geiger and Meueleman, 2016) despite the fact that official figures show that fraud is very low and that in fact more money is lost via mistakes in the system, although even this remains a small fraction of the overall spending on 'welfare' (DWP, 2016). It is also the case that most people associate the biggest spend on 'welfare' as being out-of-work benefits rather than pensions, and that they also over-estimate how much money those on out-of-work benefits receive (Baumberg Geiger and Meueleman, 2016).

Austerity adds a final layer of insult to injury for those on low incomes and all the evidence suggests that 'welfare' reforms are leading to devastating impacts (Cooper and Whyte, 2017). Burnett refers to the 'institutionally produced hatred' (Burnett, 2017, p 217) that has been directed towards claimants of 'welfare' as fuelling an 'austerity politics' (p 217) that means that people forced to engage with the

References

Aguiar, L. (2006) 'Janitors and sweatshop citizenship in Canada', *Antipode*, vol 38, no 3, pp 440–61.

Aitchison, G. (2013) 'Councillor in attack on foodbank', *The Press* (York), 3 January, www.yorkpress.co.uk/news/10138097.Councillor_in_attack_on_food_bank/

Alcock, P. (2006) *Understanding poverty*, Basingstoke: Palgrave Macmillan.

Allen, K., Mendick, H., Harvey, L. and Ahmed, A. (2015) 'Celebrity motherhood and the cultural politics of austerity', *Feminist Media Studies*, vol 15, no 6, pp 907–25.

Allwood, J. (2016) *A bright future for UK steel*, Cambridge, Cambridge University https://www.cam.ac.uk/system/files/a_bright_future_for_uk_steel_2.pdf

Archer et al (2007) '"University's not for me, I'm a Nike person": Urban working class young people's negotiation of "style", identity and educational engagement', *Sociology*, vol 4, no 2, pp 219–37.

Archer, L., Hollingworth, S. and Mendick, H. (2010) *Urban youth and schooling*, Milton Keynes: Open University Press.

Arni, P., Lalive, R. and Van Ours, J.C. (2013) 'How effective are unemployment benefit sanctions: looking beyond unemployment exit', *Journal of Applied Econometrics*, vol 28, no 7, pp 1153–78.

Ashton, J. et al (2014) 'An open letter to Prime Minister David Cameron on food poverty in the UK', open letter signed by 170 signatories, *The Lancet*, www.thelancet.com/journals/lancet/article/PIIS0140-6736(14)60536-5/fulltext

ATD Fourth World (2016) *Towards sustainable development that leaves no one behind: The challenge of the post 2015 agenda*, London: ATD Fourth World.

Atkinson, R., Burrows, R. and Rhodes, D. (2016) 'Capital city? London's housing market and the "super rich"' in I. Hay and J. Beaverstock (eds) *International handbook of wealth and the super rich*, London: Edward Elgar, pp 225–43.

Atkinson, W. (2010) *Class, individualisation and late modernity: In search of the reflexive worker*, Basingstoke, Palgrave MacMillan

Atkinson, W. (2015) *Inequality: What can be done*, Boston, MA: Harvard University Press.

Atkinson, W., Roberts, S. and Savage, M. (2012) *Class inequality in austerity Britain*, Basingstoke: Palgrave Macmillan.

Back, L. (2014) *A fairy tale from New Addington*, Case Stories, 24 January, www.case-stories.org/blog/2014/1/24/a-fairytale-from-new-addington-les-back

Ball, S., Maguire, M. and McCrae, S. (2000) *Choice, pathways and transitions post-16: New youth, new economies in the city*, London, Routledge.

Bambra, C. (2016) *Health divides: Where you live can kill you*, Bristol: Policy Press.

Barnes, M.C., Gunnell, D., Davies, R.L., Hawton, K., Kapur, N., Potokar, J.P. and Donovan, J.C. (2016) 'Understanding vulnerability to self harm in times of economic hardship and austerity', *BMJ open*, http://bmjopen.bmj.com/content/6/2/e010131

Barr, B. et al (2015) 'First, do no harm: are disability assessments associated with adverse trends in mental health? A longitudinal ecological study', *Journal of Epidemiology and Community Health*, vol 70, no 4, pp 339-45.

Bauman, Z. (1998) *Work, consumerism and the new poor*, Buckingham: Open University Press.

Bauman, Z. (2013) *Does the richness of the few benefit us all?*, Cambridge: Polity.

Baumberg, B., Bell, K., Gaffney, D., Deacon, R., Hood, C. and Sage, D. (2012) *Benefit stigma in Britain*, London: Turn2US, https://wwwturn2us-2938.cdn.hybridcloudspan.com/T2UWebsite/media/Documents/Benefits-Stigma-in-Britain.pdf

Baumberg Geiger, B. and Meuleman, B. (2016) 'Beyond "mythbusting": how to respond to myths and perceived undeservingness in the British benefits system', *Journal of Poverty and Social Justice* [online] vol 24, no 3, pp 291-306, http://doi.org/10.1332/175982716X14721954314968

BBC News (2012) 'Margaret Hodge: A4e contracts must be suspended', 23 March, www.bbc.co.uk/news/av/uk-17484383/margaret-hodge-a4e-contracts-must-be-suspended

Beatty, C. and Fothergill, S. (2016) *Jobs, welfare and austerity: How the destruction of industrial Britain casts a shadow over present-day public finances*, Sheffield: CRESR, Sheffield Hallam University.

Beatty, C., Foden, M., McCarthy, L. and Reeve, K. (2015) *Benefit sanctions and homelessness: A scoping report*, London: Crisis.

Beatty, T., Blow, L. and Crossley, T. (2011) *Is there a 'heat or eat' trade-off in the UK?*, London: IFS.

Beck, U. (2002) *Individualization*, London: Sage.

Belfield, C., Cribb, J., Hood, A. and Joyce, R. (2016) *Living standards, poverty and inequality in the UK: 2016*, London: IFS.

Bell, F. (1907) *At the works*, London: Virago Press.

DWP (2015) *Benefit Cap: 200 people into work or off housing benefit every week*, London, DWP, https://www.gov.uk/government/news/benefit-cap-200-people-into-work-or-off-housing-benefit-every-week

DWP (2016) *Roll out of flagship welfare reform Universal Credit reaches historic milestone*, London, DWP, https://www.gov.uk/government/news/rollout-of-flagship-welfare-reform-universal-credit-reaches-historic-milestone

Dwyer, P. and Wright, S. (2014) 'Universal credit, ubiquitous conditionality and its implications for social citizenship', *Journal of Poverty and Social Justice*, vol 22, no 1, pp 27-35.

Edensor, T. and Millington, S. (2009) 'Illuminations, class identities and the contested landscapes of Christmas', *Sociology*, vol 43, no 1, pp 103–21.

EHRC (Equality and Human Rights Commission) (2010) *Enquiry into recruitment and employment in the meat and poultry processing sector*, London: Equality and Human Rights Commission.

EHRC (2014) *Workforce employment practices in the cleaning sector: Findings report*, London: Equality and Human Rights Commission.

Engels, F. (2009) *The condition of the working class in England*, Oxford; Oxford University.

European Commission (2016) *Commission takes action to preserve sustainable jobs and growth in Europe*, Press release, Brussels, 16 March, http://europa.eu/rapid/press-release_IP-16-804_en.htm

Evans, G. and Tilley, J. (2015) 'The new class war: excluding the working class in 21st-century Britain', *Juncture*, vol 21, no 4, pp 298–304.

Evans, G. and Tilley, J. (2017) *The new politics of class*, Oxford: Oxford University Press.

Fell, B. and Hewstone, M. (2015) *Psychological perspectives on poverty*, York: JRF.

Felstead, A., Gallie, D. and Green, A. (2015) *Unequal Britain at work*, Oxford: Oxford University Press.

Field, F. and Forsey, A. (2016) *Fixing broken Britain? An audit of working-age 'welfare' reform since 2010*, London: Civitas.

Fitzpatrick, S., Bramley, G., Sosenko, F., Blenkinsopp, J., Johnsen, S., Littlewood, M., Netto, G. and Watts, B. (2016) *Destitution in the UK*, York, JRF.

Fletcher, D., Batty, E., Flint, J.F. and McNeill, J. (2016) 'Gamers or victims of the system? Welfare reform, cynical manipulation and vulnerability', *Journal of Poverty and Social Justice*, vol 24, no 2, pp 171-185.

Frazer, N., Gutierrez, R. and Pena-Casas, R. (eds) (2011) *Working poverty in Europe: A comparative perspective*, Basingstoke, Palgrave Macmillan.

Freud, D. (2012) Interview with *The House* magazine, https://www. politicshome.com/articles/magazine/house

Gaffney, D. (2014) 'James Turner Street exists: Benefit Street doesn't', Left Foot Forward blog post, http://www.leftfootforward.org/ author/declangaffney/

Gaffney, D. and Baumberg, B. (2015) *Dismantling the barriers to social mobility*, Touchstone Extras No 12, London: Trades Union Congress.

Gallie, D. (2015) 'Class inequality at work: trends to polarization', in A. Felstead, D. Gallie and A. Green (eds) *Unequal Britain at work*, Oxford: Oxford University Press

Gamble, A. (2014) 'Austerity as statecraft', *Parliamentary Affairs*, vol 68, no 1, pp 42–58.

Garthwaite, K. (2016a) *Hunger pains: Life inside foodbank Britain*, Bristol: Policy Press.

Garthwaite, K. (2016b) 'Stigma, shame and people like us: an ethnographic study of foodbank use in the UK', *Journal of Poverty and Social Justice*, vol 24, no 3, pp 277–89.

Garnham, A. (2010) Interview with Alison Garnham, Chief Executive of Child Poverty Action Group, *Children and Young People Now*, 18 October.

Giddens, A. (1999) *Runaway world: How globalization is reshaping our lives*, London: Profile.

Gillies, V. (2005) 'Raising the meritocracy: parenting and the individualisation of class', *Sociology*, vol 39, no 5, pp 835–853.

Goodley, S. (2016) 'Mike Ashley running Sports Direct like a "Victorian workhouse"', *Guardian*, 22 July.

Goodwin, M. and Heath, O. (2016) *Brexit vote explained: Poverty, low skills and lack of opportunities*, York: JRF.

Gordon, L. (1998) 'How welfare became a dirty word', *New Global Development*, vol 14, no 1, pp 1–14.

Gordon, D. et al (2013) *The impoverishment of the UK*, http://poverty. ac.uk/system/files/attachments/The_Impoverishment_of_the_UK_ PSE_UK_first_results_summary_report_March_28.pdf

Goulden, C. (2010) *Cycles of poverty, unemployment and low pay*, York JRF.

Goulden, C. (2013) 'There is much more to poverty than addiction to drugs and alcohol', http://discoversociety.org/2017/02/01/suicides-linked-to-austerity-from-a-psychocentric-to-a-psychopolitical-autopsy/.

Graham, H. (2006) 'Socio-economic change and inequalities in men and women's health in the UK', in S. Nettleton and U. Gustafsson (eds) *The sociology of health and illness reader*, Cambridge: Polity..

Shildrick, T. (2000) 'Youth culture, the 'underclass' and social exclusion', *Scottish Youth Issues Journal*, vol 1, no 1.

Shildrick, T. (2002) 'Young people, illicit drug use and the question of normalisation', *Journal of Youth Studies*, vol 5, no 1, pp 35–48.

Shildrick, T. (2006) 'Youth culture, subculture and the importance of neighbourhood', *Young*, vol 14, no 2, pp 61–74.

Shildrick, T. (2015) *Steel work closures and the importance of class and place*, London: CLASS, http://classonline.org.uk/blog/item/steelwork-closures-and-the-importance-of-class.

Shildrick, T. (2018 forthcoming) 'Lessons from Grenfell: poverty propaganda, stigma and class power', in I. Tyler and S. Slater (eds) *The sociology of stigma*, Sociological Review Monograph Series.

Shildrick, T. and MacDonald, R. (2008) 'Understanding youth exclusion: critical moments, social networks and social capital', *Youth and Policy*, vol 99, pp 46–64.

Shildrick, T. and MacDonald, R. (2013) 'Poverty talk: how people experiencing poverty deny their poverty and why they blame the poor', *The Sociological Review*, vol 61, no 2, pp 285–303.

Shildrick, T., MacDonald, R., Webster, C. and Garthwaite, K. (2010) *The low pay, no pay cycle: Understanding recurrent poverty*, York: JRF.

Shildrick, T., MacDonald, R., Webster, C. and Garthwaite, K. (2012a) *Poverty and insecurity: Life in low pay, no pay Britain*, Bristol: Policy Press.

Shildrick, T., MacDonald, R., Furlong, A., Roden, J. and Crow, R. (2012b) *Are cultures of worklessness passed down the generations?*, York: JRF.

Shildrick, T., MacDonald, R. and Furlong, A. (2016) 'Not single spies but in battalions: a critical, sociological engagement with the idea of so-called "Troubled Families"', *The Sociological Review*, early view online (October), http://onlinelibrary.wiley.com/doi/10.1111/1467–954X.12425/full

Sinfield, A. (1975) 'We are the people and they the poor: a comparative view of poverty research', *Irish Journal of Sociology*, vol 4, no 1, pp 3-25.

Skeggs, B. (1997) *Formations of class and gender: Becoming respectable*, London: Sage.

Skeggs, B. (2005) *Class, self and culture*, London: Routledge.

Skeggs, B. (2010) 'Class, culture and morality: Legacies and logics in the space for identification', in M. Weatherell and C. Talpade Mohantry (eds) *The Sage Handbook of Identities*, London, Sage

Skeggs, B. (2017) *A crisis in humanity: What everyone with parents is likely to face in the future*, blog for *Sociological Review*, https://www.thesociologicalreview.com/blog/a-crisis-in-humanity-what-everyone-with-parents-is-likely-to-face-in-the-future.html.

Slater, T. (2012) 'The myth of "Broken Britain": Welfare reform and the production of ignorance', *Antipode*, vol 46, no 4, pp 948–64.

Smith, D. (2005) *On the margins of inclusion: Changing labour markets and social exclusion in London*, Bristol: Policy Press.

Smith, N. and Middleton, S. (2007) *Poverty dynamics research in the UK*, York: JRF.

Soubry, A. (2013) 'Poor families tend to be obese', https://www.standard.co.uk/news/uk/public-health-minister-anna-soubry-poor-families-tend-to-be-obese-8462536.html.

Standing, G. (2010) *The precariat*, London: Bloomsbury.

Standing, G. (2014) *A precariat charter: From denizens to citizens*, London and New York: Bloomsbury.

Standing, G. (2016) *The corruption of capitalism: Why rentiers thrive and work does not pay*, London: Biteback Publishing.

Stanley, J. (2015) *How propaganda works*, Princeton, NJ: Princeton University Press.

Stanley, L. (2015) *What six public opinion graphs tell us about austerity*, Sheffield: Sheffield Political Economy Research Institute.

Stone, J (2016) 'Scrapping the Human Rights Act will help protect human rights, Attorney General says', *The Independent*, 25 February, www.independent.co.uk/news/uk/politics/scrapping-the-human-rights-act-will-help-protect-human-rights-attorney-general-says-a6894966.html

Strelitz, J. and Lister, R. (eds) (2008) *Why money matters: Family income, poverty and children's lives*, London: Save the Children, pp 115–24.

Taylor-Gooby, P. (2013) *The double crisis of the 'welfare' state and what we can do about it*, Basingstoke: Palgrave Macmillan.

Taylor-Gooby, P. (2017) 'Redoubling the crises of the welfare state: the impact of Brexit on UK welfare politics', *Journal of Social Policy*, vol 46, no 4, pp 815–36.

Thatcher, M. (1978) 'The Thatcher philosophy', interview with the *Catholic Herald*, 22 December, www.margaretthatcher.org, cited in O. Jones (2012) *Chavs: The demonization of the working class* (2nd edn), London: Verso.

Thatcher, M. (1984) Remarks on Orgreave picketing (30 May), Thatcher Archives, https://www.margaretthatcher.org/document/105691

Thompson, S. (2015) *The low-pay, no-pay cycle*, York: JRF.

Townsend, P. (1975) *Sociology and Social Policy*, London, Lane Publishers

Townsend, P. (1979) *Poverty in the United Kingdom,* London, Allen Lane

Todd, S. (2014) *The people: The rise and fall of the working class 1910–2010*, Murray Publishers.